AFRICAN SOCIETY TODAY
The African worker

FEB 1 1 2004

AFRICAN SOCIETY TODAY

General editor: ROBIN COHEN

Advisory editors: O. Aribiah, Jean Copans,
Paul Lubeck, Philip M. Mbithi, M. S. Muntemba,
O. Nnoli, Richard Sandbrook

The series has been designed to provide scholarly, but lively and up-to-date, books, likely to appeal to a wide readership. The authors will be drawn from the field of development studies and all the social sciences, and will also have had experience of teaching and research in a number of African countries.

The books will deal with the various social groups and classes that comprise contemporary African society and successive volumes will link with previous volumes to create an integrated and comprehensive picture of the African social structure.

Also in the series

Farm labour. KEN SWINDELL
Migrant laborers. SHARON STICHTER
The politics of Africa's economic stagnation.
RICHARD A. SANDBROOK
Inequality in Africa: political elites, peasants and the poor.
E. WAYNE NAFZIGER
African capitalism: the struggle for ascendency. PAUL KENNEDY

THE AFRICAN WORKER

BILL FREUND

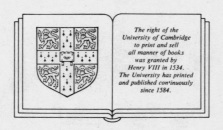

The right of the
University of Cambridge
to print and sell
all manner of books
was granted by
Henry VIII in 1534.
The University has printed
and published continuously
since 1584.

CAMBRIDGE UNIVERSITY PRESS

CAMBRIDGE

NEW YORK NEW ROCHELLE MELBOURNE SYDNEY

Published by the Press Syndicate of the University of Cambridge
The Pitt Building, Trumpington Street, Cambridge CB2 1RP
32 East 57th Street, New York, NY 10022, USA
10 Stamford Road, Oakleigh, Melbourne 3166, Australia

First published 1988

Printed in Great Britain at the University Press, Cambridge

British Library cataloguing in publication data
Freund, Bill
The African worker. – (African society today)
1. Africa south of the Sahara. Employment. Labour, to 1987
1. Title   11. Series
331′.0967

Library of Congress cataloguing in publication data
Freund, Bill.
The African worker.
(African society today)
Bibliography.
Includes index.
1. Labor and laboring classes – Africa.   1. Title. 11. Series.
HD8776.5.F74   1988   305.5′62′096   87-38102

ISBN 0 521 30758 9 hard covers
ISBN 0 521 31491 7 paperback

SE

❦ CONTENTS ❦

Preface   *page* vii

1   The historiography of labour   1
2   The material basis for an African working
    class   25
3   Culture, community and class   45
4   Wage labour, non-wage labour and the total
    sphere of production   63
5   Trade unions, workers and the state   91
6   Labour in an industrialised society: the
    South African case   110
7   Labour, the development process and social
    change   139
8   A guide to the literature on labour in Africa   144

Bibliography   166
Index   195

❧ PREFACE ❧

The African worker is intended as a synthesis considering issues and debates from the work of many writers on labour history and labour studies in Africa. The development of a particular critical literature, spanning a number of disciplines, is critically considered. In some respects, the concerns of the past generation have been to align the understanding of labour issues in Africa with those more generally in the modern world. In others, the emphasis remains on the specific and African. Both directions clearly emerge here. The bibliographical essay, as well as the bibliography itself, is meant to point readers further who want a higher order of detail, a regional focus or a more thorough-going theoretical treatment of all or some of the relevant issues.

This book developed out of ideas put forward in a review essay which was commissioned by the Social Science Research Council of New York and the African Studies Association of the USA. It was published in the *African Studies Review* (27 (2) 1984) and reproduced the following year by the *Newsletter of International Labour Studies* in the Netherlands. That essay was much more confined to being a review of the scholarly literature. The minor attempts in it at coverage of North Africa have largely been abandoned here while I have provided far more material on South Africa.

That essay contained acknowledgements to numerous scholars who provided input at the request of the Social Science Research Council as well as Boston friends kind enough to help as critical readers at an earlier stage and they deserve thanks here. However, this book wishes to acknowledge specifically the helpful comments of readers in Durban, Jeremy Grest, Sheila Meintjes and Mike Morris, as well as the history seminar at the University of South Africa in Pretoria, where a chapter was presented. Mrs Norma Hatcher made the transformation from my drafts into a typescript a thankfully painless operation for me through her efficient labours.

I should like to dedicate this book to my many South African friends who have, as intellectuals, through their debates and engagement, made a critical and unique contribution to the renaissance of the South African trade-union movement in the last fifteen years.

~ 1 ~

THE HISTORIOGRAPHY OF LABOUR

The lives of Africans can be understood in many ways, through religious beliefs and practices, through cultural responses and creativity, through political life and authority, through the structures and contradictions of village and family. Kinship, ritual, art forms all may seem appropriate avenues into the study of African society. However, economic practices and relationships have also been fundamental, linked as they are to these other aspects of social being. The African has always been an economic person. If students of pre-colonial Africa have tended to neglect economic questions, it has had more to do with their own preoccupations and needs than to the potential of the subject.

Before the colonial conquests of the late nineteenth century just as much as after, human labour rested at the base of conflicts over power and possibilities of material development. It is often said that pre-colonial African societies were *subsistence* economies where people produced solely in order to survive and local communities were essentially self-sufficient in providing what they needed. There can be little dispute that the concept of subsistence is correct in so far as it focusses on survival and the basic needs of social as well as biological reproduction, that is to say of the lineage or community as well as the family and the individual. However, it is quite wrong to assume from this that African cultivators or producers always lived at a marginal level

I

with no technological capacity to produce more than a bare minimum. They acquired a complex and detailed understanding of their own environment. In fact, most African communities were able to produce a fairly substantial surplus and have been involved over the past two millennia in extensive networks of exchange.

If some exchange involved the transmission of luxury goods, the basic stock-in-trade, repeated in region after region, consisted of the satisfaction of fairly fundamental needs: dried fish rich in protein, salt, pottery, iron and iron ware. Onto this humble pattern one can as well find appended a more glamorous trade in beads, art objects or precious metals. In much of sub-Saharan Africa, exchange was structured for centuries through the evolution of specific exchange means accepted over many states and societies (cloth, metal tokens, shells) and through the emergence of specialised trading communities following long-established trade routes. Specialisation in food production characterised parts of Mediterranean Africa in the Ancient World. Thus parts of Tunisia constituted a granary for the cities of the Roman Empire. By the nineteenth century, certain areas in tropical Africa, also typically rather intensely integrated into world trade networks, similarly were able to concentrate on quite specialised market production. In parts of the Niger River delta, communities of fishermen, later evolving into traders in response to the rise of Atlantic slaving, relied entirely on inland communities to supply them with staple foods. In Sierra Leone and Senegambia systematic cultivation developed to service the slave ships. Grain exports intended for the oases of the Sahara were grown in desert-side communities of the Sahel. The slaves of Zanzibar clove plantations (as well as their masters and the urban commercial community of the islands of the East Africa littoral) relied on food produced by other slaves on mainland grain and rice farms.

The nature of surplus production was shaped by the vagaries both of social and natural environment. The danger of a severe drought was always there for most of the continent. Long-distance commerce was nowhere so well-developed as to eliminate the threat. The kind of crops grown and the importance laid on storage ultimately reflected the tyranny of what the Shona of contemporary Zimbabwe call *shangwa*, drought (Palmer and Parsons, 1977). The disposal of a surplus always is problematic in agrarian society and particularly in one with only a limited commercial nexus. In the end it does largely remain true that production in Africa was for use, rather than exchange, value and that commerce itself was intended to extend the reproduction of the producing household. Communities did not depend on goods brought in from outside for their survival.

Production in Africa cannot be divorced from questions of power and inequality. There is a conventional portrait that has long existed in Western scholarship, but which also serves the political interests of many African intellectuals and politicians, which stresses the undifferentiated and egalitarian nature of African society. In this view, the African king or ruler, where he existed, held power largely through spiritual or ideological forms of control rather than because of the constraints of the political economy. The Swedish political scientist Goran Hyden, trying to provide a political and social explanation of the current African agrarian crisis, has synthesised a sophisticated and contemporary version of this argument in hypothesising an 'economy of affection' that reigned and continues to reign in tropical Africa where peasants are able to resist the dictates of artificial, colonially created state apparatuses with relative impunity – 'holding the barriers against capitalist penetration' (Hyden, 1980, 237).

Of course, consensus would never consider that the fer-

tile stretches of North Africa belong to the economy of
affection; the Nile peasantry must be as accustomed to a
state apparatus as any people on earth. However, it is not
often realised how much of tropical Africa (and on the
whole, a growing portion) also experienced the weight of
economically effective states in the last centuries before
colonial conquest. We must consider in addition to Egypt,
the lands of the upper Nile and the peasantries of the Horn
of Africa, the world expanding out from the islands off the
East African coast and a variety of agrarian societies in
savanna and forest West Africa. Most Africans by the late
nineteenth century were the subjects (or prey) of strong
states. On the very edge of Tanzania, the East African
country about which Hyden is most expert, Claudine Vidal
has created a picture of life in the interlacustrine kingdom of
Rwanda, where a densely peopled region provided very
unequal access to land and the tools to work it, where a
clearly demarcated ruling class were able to control people's
loyalties through their ability to regulate the system and
where the ruling house clearly represented that class interest
(Vidal, 1974). In the emirates of what is today the northern
part of Nigeria, the court and its minions extracted from the
talakawa (the Hausa word for free commoners) a surplus
that British conquerors found perfectly respectable by the
standards of Asian despotisms (Freund and Shenton, 1979).
Such were conditions in the most populous sector of the
savanna belt south of the Sahara, an area with a great, long-
term historic importance and impact.

What does need perhaps to be considered is the extent to
which many African rulers or ruling strata depended on
some form of personal ownership of individuals, captives
and their descendants, in order to extract labour and thus
wealth from their subjects. The prevalence of slavery, the
use of slave armies and slave estates can be meshed with an
emphasis by some writers on the predatory and thus ex-

traneous nature of many early African states and by others on the command of long-distance trade as a means of acquiring wealth that could not come from the systematic despoliation of a peasantry (Goody, 1971; Coquery-Vidrovitch, 1976). Slaves could be integrated socially in such complex ways that one cannot actually consider them a 'class' but their subjugation, even if it could not be maintained for generations, provided a means of extracting surplus and obedience from the peasantry more generally. Far to the south, in fairly recent times, we have evidence of how the succession of Nguni-speaking warrior chiefs in what is now Natal, culminating in Shaka Zulu, cleverly inserted their power over the reproductive capacity of age-grades, obliging men to do service for them before they could marry, as a means of founding some measure of state authority in a part of Africa where little material differentiation had historically existed (Guy, 1979). In much of Africa, therefore, an economy of depredation and intervention accompanied an economy of affection but it did not lead so firmly as in Zanzibar, in Hausaland, in highland Ethiopia or in the Nile Delta, to a clearly understood class society based on differentiated access to the means of production.

There is an increasingly generalised recognition today, partly in response to feminist scholarship, that household production itself requires differentiated treatment. The African household was not simply a sharing environment where everyone ate equitably from the same bowl. There has been an attempt, in fact, to register this understanding rigorously in terms of hierarchy and exploitation through the formulation of a distinctive lineage mode of production where the male elder ultimately controlled and exploited a surplus produced by juniors and females of all ages, as well as by slaves and others who had a minimum of rights within the household (Meillassoux, 1972, 1981).

It must be said, however, that the rights of male elders to appropriate surplus in African societies varied immensely as does the right of African women to a share of what they produce themselves (Guyer, 1982). The lineage mode of production model holds up well for some places and historic situations and not at all for others. Even where the patriarchal pattern is most deeply entrenched, however, it is not entirely clear how we could provide a completely convincing economic explanation for the power that is being exerted by elders. The heavy labour burden on younger women is however an extremely commonly observed phenomenon.

New research into labour in pre-colonial African society reflects new directions in African history and anthropology over the years since 1970. Until that time, questions about human labour were not fundamental to research on African households or African states. Indeed the literature that has developed has often been essentially intended to move us to consider the state or the relation between the sexes or the nature of kinship, questions which have long exercised scholarship in Africa. It can very readily be argued that even current scholarship, while providing some effective descriptions of African labour systems (Cooper, 1977), is often far too ready to move from generalisations about labour to the apparently 'broader' issues.

A much-discussed example lies in the elegantly conceived and theoretically penetrating work of the French historian Emmanuel Terray, whose study of the Abron kingdom of Gyaman led him to explain the basis of power in the kingdom on the royally controlled gold mines worked by slaves (Terray, 1974). In fact, it is not very clear that the systematic exploitation by slaves of relatively deep-level mines was actually very important in Gyaman (and West African) mineral production and export. According to a critic, 'traditional gold mining was carried out mainly by free family labour with slaves used as an adjunct to the kin-based labour unit' (Dumett, 1979, 64). Terray is so focussed on the question of the state that he tends to move away far too quickly from the labour process and its ramifications.

There is much that is unknown and remains for historians to explore on the conceptual complexities of labour organisation and its relation to social structure in pre-colonial Africa, as hopefully has been indicated. However, it was only with the advent of European imperialism in Africa that we can talk about a consistent attitude towards labour in the scholarly literature which ultimately feeds into contemporary debate and relates to an historiography of labour. Broadly speaking, this literature may be periodised readily. First, there is a specifically imperial literature on labour linked to the slave-trade era, the object of the missionaries and the traders in raw materials of the nineteenth century which can be linked up to the Scramble for Africa. Secondly, colonial rule, which apparently promised the generalisation of a free labour market and the blossoming of uncoerced enterprise in Africa, proved to have a far more complicated and less happy impact and the contradictions that resulted generated an expansion of considerations about labour in colonial literature. Thirdly, from the time, roughly speaking, of World War II, late colonialism brought forth a literature on labour of considerable richness and depth that broke qualitatively, for historic reasons, with earlier assessments. Finally, independence has shifted the balance towards more political views of labour moving from an initial emphasis on the politics of trade unions to a more current one that takes a very wide-ranging view of labour issues. These phases will be considered in some detail in the pages that follow.

Early European interests in Africa were at first diverse; Europeans bought West African peppers, products of the hunt such as ivory and tropical woods when available near the coast, searched for precious metals and tried to establish alliances against the Turkish enemy. However, by contrast with Mediterranean Africa, which provided Europe with some desirable manufactured luxuries – carpets and leather goods – tropical Africa in general did not. Gold was one of the few products from Africa involving human application and skilled labour that was desired by Europeans when the voyages of discovery opened the shores of the entire continent to commercially minded travellers from the fifteenth century onwards.

Commercial links between Africa and Europe became more and more dominated by one notorious exchange, the sale of African slaves at the ports to those who arranged their passage across the Atlantic Ocean to plantation colonies in the New World. By the middle of the seventeenth century, with the systematic establishment of sugar plantations in the Caribbean region, the slave traffic became massive and remained so for the following two hundred years. Some ten to twenty million slaves were during this era taken from their normal existence with the intention of shipping them to America.

The impact of the slave trade on Africa itself is debatable, particularly with regard to population. Many writers have assumed that depopulation brought about by slaving must have had a major effect on the economic underdevelopment of Africa through the sheer loss of manpower. Those who have tried to establish findings with more precision have, however, generally come up with contrary results. The slave trade worked in very uneven ways. Some regions where the state used the trade to its advantage became in conventional terms richer and more populous through its workings, although ultimately it cannot be said that they were not just as much industrially underdeveloped when confronted with capitalist Europe in time. There was a strong tendency for male slaves to be sold to the Atlantic trade; women slaves, who did much or most of the productive labour and who had a greater commercial value, were largely kept in Africa to enrich powerful households. There is moreover no correlation between the concentration of population in Africa since reliable records can be used as evidence, and the extent of slaving; some of the major sources of slaves are extremely heavily peopled areas while other areas seem lightly peopled because of ecologically unfavourable conditions. Given our inability, finally, to know much about the population concentration or growth rates of Africa in the past, the whole subject is likely to remain highly uncertain. Much of the significance of the slave trade was not to be measured in terms of labour gained or lost to America or Africa, but in terms of a form of commercialisation with the consequent ties built up or intensified over long distances, the prevalence of armed men disrupting the more peaceful patterns of development and the assistance given to the formation or growth of what Walter Rodney called 'social oppression' (Rodney, 1966).

What must be stressed for the moment is that Europeans found little use for the application of human labour to production in Africa itself. To this there was one exception: the Dutch colony at the southernmost extremity of Africa which expanded into the interior during the late seventeenth and eighteenth centuries (Elphick & Giliomee, 1979). By American standards, this was a small-scale colony of very modest wealth that expanded only slowly; its successful exploitation even then depended, much as in America, on the importation of outside labour – slaves from elsewhere in Africa, from Madagascar and from Asia in particular, as well as from the direct immigration of Europeans.

During the nineteenth century, the Atlantic slave trade came to an end, excoriated by reformers in Europe whose ban was enforced by the energetic naval patrols of the first industrial capitalist nation, Britain. Historians debate the cause for this dramatic shift and the rather sudden turn in moral opinion against slavery. Although the sugar island colonies of Britain were less profitable than they had been in an earlier phase, when the soil was richer and sugar scarcer in Europe, it is increasingly acknowledged that slavery was profitable in many places until abolition and that it could be adapted to some extent to all kinds of industrial situations. However, an ideology of free wage labour, the essence of capitalist economic and social relations, achieved greater and greater hegemony in the nineteenth century. Only wage labour provided the generalised incentives and internalised capitalist values which made these relations entirely viable.

The abolition of the slave trade was followed by the full-scale abolition of slavery in the New World colonies, in the British Empire in 1833, in the French Empire in 1848, in the USA in 1865, in Cuba in 1880 and in Brazil in 1888. The British forced the Zanzibari state, which sold slaves primarily to the non-capitalist world of the Middle East and western Asia, to close down its infamous slave market in 1873 and eventually to abolish statutory slavery, even though it was slave plantations of clove trees that made the prosperity of the sultanate. Indeed, the zeal for abolition and anti-slavery spread to Africa itself. The evils of slaving and slavery were a major theme in the propaganda of imperialism as Europe turned to carve up Africa and annex its peoples in the 1880s and 1890s. Yet it would be a mistake to see this propaganda as justification for conquest alone or a weapon in a war to get God on the colonists' side.

It was in fact genuinely believed that the labour system in Africa needed to be transformed in order to create a productive, prosperous world with which European capitalists could do good business. In West Africa, Anthony Hopkins has systematically related the intensifying demands for European political intervention to the problems which

European and coastal merchants felt in penetrating the interior markets and supply sources profitably (Hopkins, 1973). The Scramble for West Africa is convincingly explained by him in terms of a commercial crisis. In Central and East Africa, equivalent commercial interests were less developed. It is hard to extricate European conquest there from the propaganda of the Livingstones and Stanleys about the depredations of the slave trade and the cruelties of African rule whose elimination would pave the way for prosperity and propriety.

In southern Africa, the imperatives for imperial expansion were rather more obvious. From the time of the discovery of substantial mineral deposits with the related need to discipline and organise a substantial workforce, there were important forces calling for a new British-run political order that would unify a variety of territories under the Crown and unify a 'Native' policy – labour recruitment and organisation policy – for the entire sub-continent. Already in the late 1870s, a Confederation scheme to place the trekker Boer republics under British control and to pick fights with the remaining independent African states in the area has been so interpreted by historian Norman Etherington (Etherington, 1979). The Boer War can also be placed in the context of the needs of mining capital for a political environment that could actually suit the immense demands for labour, a systematic cheap food supply, a comprehensive urbanisation programme and other essentials called forth by the remarkable development of the Witwatersrand goldfield from 1886 onwards (Marks and Trapido, 1979).

In most of Africa, however, there was nothing like a paying proposition for capital of the kind the immensely important gold mines represented. Instead, there was a generalised feeling within imperialist circles that Africa's resources could be harnessed only if labour could be developed in a more efficient manner. It was now recognised that slavery as a system brought in its wake violence, resistance and low levels of productivity. Familial household structures resisted the commercial imprecations of the market. African merchants clung to monopolies over products and routes in order to raise prices while African ruling classes took shares of the product without creating conditions suitable for the expansion of marketable wealth in return. Imperial expansion in the last quarter of the nineteenth century cannot simply be explained through economic calculation; it clearly had a wide social and cultural dimension to it but while specific conquests followed the lines of narrowly strategic or even somewhat accidental considerations at times, it is clear that the economic core of the imperial idea cannot be divorced from attitudes towards labour and the desire to transform the nature of labour in Africa.

It would seem as though colonial rule thus heralded an enlightened and benevolent era for the African as worker according to this kind of capitalist rationale. In reality, as the historian of East Africa, John Iliffe, has put it, 'low wages, long-distance migration and quasi-political restraints' formed the essence of labour policy and structure in the tropical African colonies (Iliffe in Kaniki, 1980, 301).

If the goal of colonialism was to create a more efficiently placed and willing workforce through the abolition of the slave trade, the colonialists discovered quickly those constraints which actually encouraged African ruling classes to resort to such forceful means. Indeed the periodic if rather unsystematic use of force stemmed from the weak hold such classes actually had had in the past. Particularly before World War I, the use of forced labour remained widespread in the less commercially developed parts of the continent despite the objectives that imperialism had laid out for itself. Compulsion is sometimes mistakenly associated with the settler colonies alone; actually contributions by writers in recent years on such divergent regions as the Northern Territories of the Gold Coast, Senegal, Northern Nigeria and French West and Equatorial Africa testify to its long-term and wide-spread importance (Thomas, 1973; Mason in Gutkind, Cohen and Copans, 1979; Fall, 1976/1977; 1983; Babassana, 1978; Sautter, 1967; Anouma, 1976). Where cheap labour was not systematically forthcoming, 'domestic' slavery, if not the trade in slaves, was tolerated for a long time after the conquest.

The use of force brought its own problems. Africa did not contain large populations of fit adults simply waiting for appropriate opportunities, spiced with a certain amount of coercion, to becoming increasingly productive for the profit of foreign settlers and companies. Colonial rulers found drought, disease and difficult ecological conditions continually in their path. In general, apart from the far north and south and certain sections of West Africa, before World War I, African populations were on the decline. In such lightly peopled zones as the equatorial forests, the desire to exploit African labour was tempered by an increasing fear that African labour might not survive the dose of exploitation to which it was being exposed. Until 1908, much of central Africa was under the thumb of the personal regime of the King of the Belgians, Léopold II, and his concession companies. The Congo 'Free State' even today has left traces of the memory of a system of enormous cruelty and short-term exploitation, immortalised by Joseph Conrad in his novella, *The Heart of Darkness*, which brought about massive depopulation during the period when 'red rubber' quotas were being demanded in the forests. This was apparently the epitome of a short-sighted regime that failed to treat its human 'resources' with a minimum of respect; in reality harshly won profits from the rubber trade actually financed the establishment of a transport system that evacuated copper, diamonds, gold and other mineral wealth from the centre of the continent to the enormous profit of Belgian capital once the state had appropriated the private royal regime and created a more effective basis of labour exploitation.

Along with the actual cruelties that forced labourers might suffer, colonial ideologues feared that the absence of productive workers would upset the delicate balance of agrarian life, already forced to operate in what Europeans came to realise was a very difficult natural environment in the first place. Colonial rulers were more and more conscious of the need to preserve the agrarian base as a source of social and political, as well as economic, stability in Africa. Such an influential tome as Lord Lugard's *Dual Mandate in Tropical Africa* (1929) emphasised the balancing act that imperialism needed to perform: striking a path between coercion and free labour, prising workers loose from the bosom of the 'economy of affection' while still retaining a viable peasant self-sufficiency. Even a decade later, William Macmillan emphasised that 'it is in fact a familiar complaint that the crude labour demands of the industries which ought to be the economic salvation of Africa are having a withering rather than a helpful influence' (Macmillan, 1938, 55).

Temporary labour migration on a large scale seemed a way of dealing with these contradictions. It made possible the rapid extension of wage labour accompanied by the survival of earlier forms of subsistence and the cultural and social values that went with it in the feeder regions. Migration had the advantage for capital of reducing wage costs and for the state in avoiding the expenditures as well as the social menace of large-scale proletarianisation. From the ground level, it looked rather different. The actual impact of migration, its relation to coercion, to existing agrarian possibilities and to social relationships in the countryside varied tremendously (Crush, 1984). Debate developed within the colonial literature that picked up on aspects of the migrancy system.

This debate became much sharper in the 1940s when academic writing on African labour started to change fairly rapidly. The war not only intensified the growth of African wage labour greatly, it appeared to witness a transition to a much larger permanent African urban population. Whatever the links of this population to the countryside, it was burgeoning as never before and the demands for basic facilities for the survival of the working population in the harsh and competitive urban environment were pressing. Yet it was now much more feasible to argue for ending a migrant system and allowing African family life to develop outside the agrarian milieu.

The last generation of European colonialism introduced new ideological and social directions. After a long phase of international trade recession and protectionist competition, world trade grew quickly and prices for colonial produce were good. There was money available for physical and social infrastructure, the construction of which was linked to promoting a more skilled, healthy, stabilised working population that could lift Africa out of poverty and stagnation. Rhetoric along these lines often contained more smoke than fire. Often far less innovative than the ideologues claimed, the kind of development that did occur stood more in line with the older forms of colonial exploitation, for instance in the emphasis on road and harbour construction.

Yet the literature on labour became much more complex and involved new issues. It moved away from the two axes of stability, depopulation and the simple issue of coercion. The literature on migration changed particularly rapidly and acquired sophistication.

During the 1940s, some writers tried to argue systematically that the massive labour migration issuing forth from some parts of the continent, for instance rural south-central

Africa, both led to the break-up of family life and to the dissolution of pre-capitalist social bonds (Read, 1942). In Northern Rhodesia, a colony deeply affected by the spectacular development of copper mining in the decade before the war, Godfrey and Monica Wilson emphasised that the labour migrant population deserved the right to a stabilised life in the towns (Wilson, 1941; Wilson and Wilson, 1945).

Other researchers explored different facets of oscillating migration. Another study of Northern Rhodesia, by William Watson, concluded in the late 1950s that rural life was not necessarily undercut by migrancy patterns. The failure of workers to establish themselves in the city meant that conservative rural values could be upheld and society was cushioned thereby against the drastic changes one might otherwise expect (Watson, 1958). This pattern was in fact confirmed by other studies from other parts of the continent, such as those of Walter Elkan in Uganda (Elkan, 1960) or Elliott Skinner in Upper Volta (Skinner, 1960). This conservative effect was what the state had hoped for. However, it also was clear that migrants themselves used their situation to their own advantage, in particular to resist full-scale dependence on wage labour (Schapera, 1947). Migrancy did not necessarily imply passivity or weakness. There was a sharp divide between those who saw labour migration as a disordered and unfortunate response to the needs of capital and the colonial state and those who saw it as a form of life that enabled the migrant to cope with legitimate and desirable needs for both subsistence and cash. At the end of the colonial era, a paradigmatic debate between the American and Portuguese anthropologists, Marvin Harris and A. Rita Ferreira, brought this out very clearly (Harris, 1959; Rita Ferreira, 1963). The American denounced labour migration in Mozambique as a crude form of social organisation that induced poverty and exemplified the backwardness of Portuguese colonialism; the

Portuguese emphasised its appeal to the migrants, who had been going to the gold mines of the Transvaal since before effective colonial occupation began and its legitimacy in terms of meeting their actual needs as they defined them themselves.

In the post-war years, the expansion of African wage work and the life of the workers in the towns became equally, or more than migrant labour, the focus of interest. Perhaps the most important centre for such study was in the British colony of Northern Rhodesia, at the Rhodes–Livingstone Institute, to which several famous anthropologists in succession, starting with Godfrey Wilson, were attached. Such scholars as Max Gluckman, A.L. Epstein and Clyde Mitchell all moved towards the thesis that the African worker needed serious and sympathetic treatment. To understand Africa in the new era, it was necessary to see that the Copperbelt miner was both an African and a miner. In their work, they mapped out new cultural forms such as Mitchell's study of the *kalela* dance and characteristically urban institutions such as voluntary associations, football clubs and trade unions (Mitchell, 1956; Epstein, 1958).

As anthropologists, however, they lacked a suitable framework for understanding these new social forms. The early attempts by anthropologists to understand urban man were framed, as their training reflected, by questions of kinship and *rite de passage* (Hellman, 1948). Structural functionalism had linked social phenomena together in a *tribal* unity. Now however the African was becoming 'detribalised'. That term was actually rejected by the Rhodes–Livingstone scholars. Instead they insisted that urban Africans were engaged in a process of *retribalisation*, in which the basic building blocks of the new urban society consisted of ethnically identified sub-communities. Tribalisation, according to Mitchell, 'was the most significant day-to-day category of social interaction' (Mitchell,

1956, 29). Yet in fact, his own material revealed a rather different picture in which all kinds of other forms of interaction, arguably some more important, could also be observed. These included links based on neighbourhood and workplace.

From the 1950s, social scientists showed a great interest in labour organisation. Labour unions in Africa seemed to be the link between nationalist politics and a mass, urban base. The new literature on African unions often belonged to the realm of political science and some of it was directly inspired by an intensifying Cold War competition over the affiliation of the union organisations. Much of the early literature on unions was concerned primarily with identification of names and organisations in a rough and ready classificatory system. It was assumed that the union was an arm of the nationalist movement. Strikes and union activity seemed to provide the most disciplined of the popular weapons on which nationalist politics could rest in post-independence Africa.

In practice, this missed the actual tensions that existed between union and party organisations, which tended to try to subordinate all other forces to their own ends. When independence came, and the nationalist movements became the main glue used to hold up state apparatuses, these tensions became overtly antagonistic. Radical regimes as much as conservative ones felt threatened both by trade-union autonomy and by what they thought of as unneeded economic and workplace demands. Julius Nyerere, perhaps the most influential post-independence spokesman for African nationalism, accused strikers of being exploiters. 'Strikes and go-slows at this point in time will benefit only those who wish to see the Arusha Declaration fail' (Nyerere, *Freedom and Socialism*, 1967, 313). The only really exploited Tanzanians were the peasantry. Léopold Sédar Senghor, the Senegalese president who achieved acceptance for his ruling party, the Parti Socialiste Sénégalais in the Socialist International, had a more conservative reputation but actually preached exactly the same gospel (Pfefferman, 1968). Some of the social scientists who identified with the goals of nationalism, even in radical form, took a hostile position to organised labour (Drake and Lacy, 1966; Bates, 1971).

Perhaps the most influential article written on African labour in the 1960s however had more of a debunking function. In 1964, E.J. Berg and Jeffrey Butler argued that the political importance of the trade union in contemporary Africa was very much exaggerated. It was a more narrowly economistic organisation than had been imagined, its success in improving the worker's lot was very limited and, compared to party and state, was inherently rather weak. They threw cold water on the view that the union was the 'leading edge of the nationalist movement' at the time when it seemed that the intense struggles between union and state in such countries as Nyerere's Tanzania and Nkrumah's Ghana were going irrevocably the way of the state (Berg and Butler, 1964).

Yet in the very year that Berg and Butler published, 1964, the workers in Africa's most populous country, Nigeria, went out on a successful general strike. Nigerian conditions defied what one might expect from Berg and Butler. Skilled workers who did earn far more than the national average successfully combined with very poorly paid labourers. A vigorous militancy coloured with political language survived in a state which itself was probably among the most conservative in its politics in all Africa. The big Nigerian strikes could only be explained as demands for state action; economic success required the state to move to raise wages, which it periodically did. Was this to be viewed purely in terms of state patronage or was it really a response to the force of the workers? Was this force to be comprehended in terms of brokeraged trade unions or as something rather more elemental and less organisational? An interesting set of debates ensued that began to broach these problems (Kilby, 1967; Warren, 1966, 1969; Weeks, 1968, 1971a; Berg, 1969; Cohen, 1971, 1974).

In the 1960s, there did not seem to be appropriate intellectual tools to deal with the issues of this debate and other issues linked to labour in contemporary Africa any more. The colonial issues of coercion vs. voluntary labour with their overt and heavy managerial overtones were no longer appropriate. The functionalist model of social structure did not organise the complex conflictual and historical issues well. However, the perspectives derived from political science and history closely aligned to the rise of African nationalism and the political decolonisation of the continent, were also rather inadequate. Political science offered modernisation theory, the assumption that traditional societies inevitably were becoming 'modern' societies modelled exactly on the advanced Western (or perhaps even Eastern) model. Historians, trying to celebrate the achievement of independence, insisted on seeing most phenomena of African life, particularly in the colonial period, as manifestations of nationalism and the assertion of the African persona.

It is unsurprising that a strongly felt need existed for a new way of understanding what was happening in Africa and notably for conceptualising the situation of the worker and the condition of labour. Throughout much of the world, the obvious first answer came from labour unions themselves: class analysis. Workers need to be understood as a class operating dynamically within societies based on class. However, in Africa itself, the union movement was too weak, poor, and historically new to provide its own battery of intellectuals who could issue such a perspective.

There did exist an internationalist class analysis that had

made a contribution over a long period of time to the understanding of African society although it had enjoyed little legitimacy within academic circles. As part of the turning towards alliances with nationalist anti-colonial movements in the 'East' on the part of the isolated Communist movement, a specific Comintern interest developed in understanding events in Africa. This understanding collapsed two processes: colonial oppression and class formation. Some of the early students of African society in the Soviet Union (such as the exiled Hungarian Endre Sik, later to produce a multi-volume history of Africa) lacked first-hand experience of their subject. However, there was as well a black South African Communist, Albert Nzula, whose Russian work with Potekhin and Zusmanovitch, *Forced Labour in Africa*, has recently been resuscitated and made available in English (Nzula et al., 1979).

For Nzula and his co-workers, apart from making available quite a rich variety of information in a rather different setting than that of writers such as Lugard or Macmillan, the central emphasis lies, not just on the travails of the undifferentiated 'African', but on the forging in a harsh workshop of a new class in Africa. This class was destined ultimately to lead an African revolution and prepare the way for a socialist Africa. This kind of analysis found its way to the West. The West Indian Pan-Africanist, George Padmore, originally a Communist although later intensely anti-Communist, wrote an account in 1936 of *How Britain Rules Africa*, which basically identified the entire African people as an oppressed proletariat. Jack Woddis, the British Communist Party expert on Africa, provided very valuable and detailed accounts of strikes and labour organisations in his post-war work (Woddis, 1959).

Little distinction was drawn between worker reaction and consciousness on the one hand, and nationalism and anti-colonial politics on the other. It was assumed that they just represented part of one great stream. Moreover, there was little effort made to identify the specific characteristics of proletarianisation in Africa; African events simply were made to follow, in a rather crude way, a pattern universally established under capitalism. This tradition could draw on the classic formulae of Marx in his assessment of British industrial capitalism – the process of enclosures and other state measures which evicted peasants from their own land, the establishment of a landless population desperate for wage labour to survive, their accumulation in cities and organisation first into trade unions and then, almost as by natural extension, into class-based political parties. While this formulation has an enormous historic explanatory power on a global level, it is insufficient to explain African conditions. In crude form, it was not compelling from the perspective of Africans.

Disillusionment with the classless nationalism of African politics first propelled intellectuals into pursuing class as a means of understanding labour and society in Africa in a new use of Marxist concepts. The Communist tradition has a harsh term, used by Engels but more especially by Lenin, for workers who seem prepared to compromise systematically with capitalism or 'imperialism' – labour aristocracy. The new literature on the African working class cut its teeth with attacks on the application of the idea of the labour aristocracy to uncooperative trade unions in post-colonial Africa. Instead, this wave threw a harsh light on the class character of the nationalist movements, their authoritarianism and the extent to which they masked the ascendancy of a manipulative new stratum able to seize state power on the backs of the workers. By the middle of the 1970s, a new generation of scholars had discovered an African working class and, armed with more flexible means of considering application of class consciousness, they began to change the way labour in Africa was being written about. The heterogeneous collection based on a conference in Canada, *The Development of an African Working Class*, marked one stage of acceptance of the class paradigm by academics (1975) and the militant, self-consciously radical collection, *African Labor History*, edited by Gutkind, Cohen and Copans (1979) marked a further one.

Such writers absorbed a considerable amount from the tradition of Sik and Woddis but the differences are also notable. For one thing, they have dropped the assumption that the African working class, formed as a class within the development of capitalist social and economic relations in struggle, is necessarily heading towards the creation of a particular kind of political party. There is an explicit and strong critique of African nationalism; the radical African nation–state is no longer assumed to be the object of working-class struggle. For another, the special character of *colonialism* is somewhat de-emphasised while increasing attention is paid to the particular historic forms of *capitalism* that can be observed in Africa. Finally, there is a notable emphasis on less conventional and systematically organised forms of class action in response to capital than trade union and party structures offer. Robin Cohen, referring to types of workplace action, for instance, refers to 'hidden forms of consciousness' in this respect (Cohen, 1980).

However, Cohen actually opens the door to perhaps the last subject that needs introduction here, the increasing development of a literature on labour that looks away entirely from the confrontation between capital and labour in the obviously capitalist arena, to consider the many aspects of labour which have been perhaps even more hidden. The reality of contemporary African society requires us to make sense of the total picture of what women do as well as men, of how labour is organised in agriculture as well as in industry, of what actually goes on in the many facets of what political economists have called the 'informal sector' of the economy. It is the weakest aspect of the class-based view of African labour, if less rigid than its predecessors, in that it has often expected the African worker to respond to his environment in a pre-determined way. Gutkind, Cohen and Copans for instance, specifically insisting on the revolutionary task of the African proletariat, wrote that 'What matters particularly at this juncture of class formation and action in Africa is what workers do (including Luddism), and perhaps as much, what they do not (yet) do' (Gutkind, Cohen and Copans, 1979, 17).

The remainder of this book will hopefully follow up much of the thought that this quote contains by assessing the African working class as a class but it also considers that working-class activity may not follow a predictable path; in order to understand the broad patterns of labour, we will need to understand the very uneven and often halting forms of capital penetration that workers do face and the sometimes surprising and contradictory patterns of response that they give to it.

Having said this much it might, in conclusion, be stressed that the chief patterns in the historiography covered have, broadly speaking, reflected a response by intellectuals to the dominant demands of the ruling class in different periods with an increasing admixture of attempts to move beyond a managerial perspective. The movement from the colonial questions of labour stability, wage-force creation and primitive accumulation to the current ones of trying to re-think the meaning of class in Africa has been a rapid one; attempts to re-structure African labour from the top are juxtaposed with attempts to liberate the labourer in a disconcerting mix of interventionist responses. Perhaps contemplating the disjunctures, however, starts to provide for the possibility of an understanding of the problems with which such a variety of intellectuals are wrestling.

THE MATERIAL BASIS FOR AN AFRICAN WORKING CLASS

Do African wage workers collectively form a working class? The working class is more than just the aggregate sum of individuals who work for a wage together with their dependents. The use of the idea 'class' implies a fundamental structural and, by implication, cultural body that shapes society as a whole. If capitalism has a meaning, it is as a mode of production in which wage labour is generalised within productive labour as a whole and where wage workers have no alternative to wage labour for the procurement of the necessities of life. Wage workers in productive labour in a capitalist society constitute the working class. Discussion of the communitarian, political and cultural aspects of working-class activity will be deferred. Here we first concentrate on the material essentials through an historical treatment.

With the exception of South Africa, capitalist social and economic relations have not yet been so generalised and the working class does not have such a totalising relationship to productive labour even today in sub-Saharan Africa. What are the implications of its minority situation? Classes are never fixed nor can they exist except in relation to other classes. The working class always is a class in becoming; its history is one of fluidity and uncertainty. In order to understand the African working class, we have to come to grips with the situation of workers who constitute only a section of the masses, or the working poor, in a particular society over which the hold of capitalist forces, although powerful, is apt to be quite incomplete. The African situation forces us to confront the historic truth that the working class is a long time in formation anywhere and that the history of workers in pre-capitalist societies deserves attention and respect because their situation remains immediately relevant still. It is also an error to assume that wage labour only began in Africa with capitalism. Indeed it clearly began before colonialism was imposed in the nineteenth century on most of the continent.

In many African societies, household relationships were only one determinant of power and labour organisation. Servile populations, many of whom can justly be considered as slaves, were very widespread. Various institutions of human bondage were prevalent through much of Africa especially, although far from exclusively, after the development of the Atlantic slave trade. Some of the literature on African slavery has belaboured the point repeatedly about its mildness by the standards of the New World plantations. There is little in fact to suggest that it was a particularly benign institution or that the slaves were generally pleased with it. However, it is important to recognise that slavery did not function primarily as a labour system. Slaves usually did work much like that of other dependent members of the household. Women were systematically more highly prized and sold for more goods or money than men; their children by free men were generally free. Slaves worked in the household and in the fields; they traded and they fought as soldiers. Precisely because they did not have full legitimate status within a particular lineage or household, they lay outside a normal system of rights that the community recognised. Africa yields examples both of areas where pariah status passed on over many generations of slaves, and others where a process of fairly rapid assimilation occurred. Assimilation was typical both in relatively undifferentiated societies where the capacity to create a permanent outsider caste was just not there and in rapidly expanding slaving societies, like those that flourished in the Congo basin and in the Niger Delta in the heyday of the slave trade. In every case, though, slavery ultimately depended on continual raiding and replenishing through warfare. This is the argument made particularly by M.I. Finley in conceptualising the slave mode of production as it existed in ancient Rome.

To what extent did slaves form a class in pre-colonial Africa? There are a limited number of accepted examples where slave plantations formed a major, quite distinctive, part of the productive system. This was certainly the case in the nineteenth-century sultanate of Zanzibar, even though the ideology of the slave owners was in some respects redolent of a patriarchal pre-capitalist world (Cooper in Lovejoy, 1981). Paul Lovejoy has made an attempt to see a distinctive slave mode of production in the Sokoto caliphate in the same era derived from the intensification of commerce and specialised commodity production (Lovejoy, 1979). Nonetheless, he acknowledges that 'slaves did not constitute a class' (Lovejoy, 1979, 205). An interesting feature of slavery in some parts of Africa, for instance, in Yoruba-speaking parts of Nigeria, was the assimilation of the (consequently degraded) idea of a day labourer to that of a slave. The other side of the coin is the Yoruba proverb that translates as 'It is better to lead a comfortable or prosperous life as a slave than to be a wretched freeborn' (Agiri in Lovejoy, 1981, 135). Slaves inevitably lacked insider status within a world whose corporate legitimacy was defined in terms of full household membership and descent. In addition, as in the Hausa world which Lovejoy writes about, there was at least some relation between the commonness of slave ownership and the general level of monetarisation and availability of labour prepared to work for cash.

In the western part of West Africa, however, there are

also communities that are usually described as castes because they are endogamous and hierarchically ranked.
These communities are occupationally specific; they included warriors, blacksmiths, weavers and leather-workers
but perhaps the most famous of them are the *griots*, or
praisesingers. It has been suggested that the caste system
emerged in its final form to serve the old ruling classes and
the state in Senegambia and the upper Niger valley. These
could separate significant communities out from the surrounding peasantry to their advantage (Diop, 1981).

From the sixteenth to the nineteenth centuries, it is possible to witness in many regions an intensifying commercialisation of the economy as international trade channels
became more important and some form of money exchange
more and more important to Africans. The combination of
money values and the growing presence of people at least
partially removed from the peasant household brought
forward growing numbers of wage labourers who were
neither slaves nor caste members. Ray Kea, in his systematic
perusal of old records from the Gold Coast, has discovered
the presence of a stratum of day labourers or 'vagabones' in
the port towns consisting of between 5 and 15 per cent of the
population in the seventeenth century (Kea, 1983, 41). They
were essential for such work as stevedoring and soldiering
and highly mobile, wandering from one centre to another. It
is interesting to note that this class was also to be found
inland as well. When travellers such as Heinrich Barth
reached the West African savanna from the Sahara in the
1850s, they found no difficulty in hiring employees to meet
their needs in centres such as Kano.

Where disease made impossible the use of animals for
carrying goods, very large numbers of porters were required. Many were slaves but by no means all. John Iliffe
records for mainland Tanzania that the great slave and
ivory caravans crucially depended on the labour of free

porters working for wages. On one great route alone, that connecting Zanzibar's mainland port of Bagamoyo with the inland trading centre of Tabora, perhaps 100,000 men were employed in this way by the middle of the nineteenth century (Iliffe, 1980, 129). Free labour was of equal importance in West African porterage.

This is not to claim that the porters of the late nineteenth century had abandoned the rural economy. On the contrary, most of them worked only seasonally and/or in conjunction with the labour of other household members who were tilling the fields on which household subsistence depended. The sexual division of labour, orientating women to work in agriculture, assisted in this kind of development in many areas. Mining in various parts of Africa had similarly developed. For ancient Zimbabwe, according to David Beach, 'the gold-mining and washing process was nearly always "seasonal" and carried out in the slack period of the agricultural cycle, to which it was definitely subordinate. There is no reliable evidence that any Shona goldfield was not primarily an agricultural area' (in Palmer and Parsons, 1977, 52).

When capitalist mining operations ensued, at first they depended on seasonal migration of enterprising workers who combined labouring on subsistence production with the satisfaction of needs in cash. The South African case is most remarkable.

With the expansion of colonial society in South Africa, the availability of cash wages grew continually. The diamond fields at Kimberley opened in 1867 held an unprecedented attraction for Africans seeking money. Parts of the northern Transvaal and southern Mozambique sent large numbers of African workers as migrants into the British South African colonies, but especially towards the mines, well before any colonial regime was in a position to direct their labour forcibly. In general, the circumstances through which such labour was offered in the nineteenth century were often not unfavourable. Money bought guns, horses and a range of goods that benefited the rural economy. By the time Portuguese rule had imposed itself in southern Mozambique in the 1890s, there were districts so given over to migrant labour that they systematically imported staple foods, so reliant were they on market relations (Harries in Marks and Rathbone, 1982).

Thus by 1900, advancing colonialism with its unprecedented demands for African labour confronted a complex situation. On the one hand, Africans in many parts of the continent were used to working for cash but they were used to doing so on their own terms which usually involved combining wage labour with other means of procuring cash and with a continued stake in subsistence production that they would fight to keep. On the other, there were certainly many regions where the imposition of coercive means was essential to prize loose a wage workforce without historic local roots whatsoever.

In many areas, so called 'floating populations' (as much the detritus of war, dislocation and personal accident as a class in the making) were recorded, that relied entirely on wage labour or the interstices of commerce for their survival. Considering the life-experiences and exploitation of 'women in peril', Marcia Wright points out that 'to be born a woman and to be dislodged from a conventional social setting in the late nineteenth century was to be exposed to the raw fact of negotiability' (Wright, 1975, 819). This was true whether or not the woman was formally a slave. The free-floating population was swelled in numbers by the more or less immediate abolition of slavery that followed the establishment of colonial power when slaves would choose to come to towns or mining camps as alternatives to the fields and homesteads of their erstwhile masters.

For African workers, total commitment to a proletarian

life-style was rarely the most attractive of options. In general, the best way to earn cash was to run some kind of business or to sell crops. Wage labour was most desirable when it could be combined with systematic exploitation of subsistence production on a household basis at the same time. One result was the massive prevalence throughout the colonial period of migrant labour. Migrant labour was not undesirable for employers: it enabled workers to be hired at lower wages and without the provision of the services and infrastructure that an urban working class would be apt to demand. However, it also suited the interests of many workers hungry for cash but who did not wish to abandon their stake in rural households.

Particularly until and during World War I (but reviving in World War II) colonial rule in Africa was marked by the prevalence of forced labour. Cultivators were forced to pay taxes in cash and participate in an extremely low-wage cash economy. Conscripted labour constructed roads and engaged in other public works. It was also directed towards private enterprise and into the hands of recruitment agencies that served the interests of employers. Forced labour (and forced military service) notoriously characterised the French colonies which were often relatively less commercialised and more lightly peopled than the British. Peasants frequently responded by seeking out more remunerative jobs where controls were less rigid, leading to a general movement of population in the West African colonies from the French to the British territories.

This migration highlights the problems that exist in a forced-labour situation for the authorities. The costs of massive coercion efforts, of co-ordinated recruitment drives, are high while the price of resistance and the scale of desertion is also large. As a result, while forms of coercion persisted in British settler colonies after World War I, in the French colonies through to World War II, and in Portuguese

Africa for longer yet, coercion itself, at its most effective, served as a means towards the creation of a situation where a workforce was actually prepared to produce itself to employers voluntarily when desired, accepting the discipline offered and demanding only a modest wage.

In Southern Rhodesia, the main thrust of colonial development for the first generation after conquest in 1890 lay in gold mining. The Rhodesian mines were scattered and not especially rich; the economic pressure on employers to stint on wages was very marked. Bad conditions and the effectiveness with which the native Shona people resisted incorporation into the labour market created a severe labour crisis for employers. These latter eventually succeeded in forming a Rhodesian Native Labour Bureau in 1903 (several times reconstituted), which managed to recruit up to 40% of the mine workers, mainly from outside Southern Rhodesia. The historian of *Chibaro* (forced labour), Charles van Onselen, devotes much attention to the abuses and poor conditions from which the conscripted or specially recruited labourers suffered (van Onselen, 1976). However, he also emphasises that the economic importance of recruitment was to serve as the wedge opening the way for the emergence of a willing, cheap labour force that appeared at the mines automatically. After 1920, *Chibaro* brought in no more than one-tenth of the workforce and the Rhodesian Native Labour Bureau could safely be dismantled in 1933. In the broad picture of things, forced labour can be seen as a rough-house method devised to press forth the commoditisation of production and conditions of reproduction in tropical Africa on a large scale.

From the point of view of the worker in colonial Africa, these conditions meant that a hierarchy of possibilities existed for obtaining cash. In general, the best choices lay in selling crops for market prices or through participation in the expanding commercial circuits. Workers were prepared to make vast journeys to obtain better situations and establish themselves in the strongest position in a job. Southern Africa contained possibilities of varying appeal. The low point on the totem pole was plantation work, particularly on the corporate estates of Mozambique or the settler farms of British Nyasaland. Van Onselen's Rhodesian gold miners were more successful but the best opportunities lay in South Africa and the Rhodesian mineowners were forced to use a variety of schemes to keep workers at their more dangerous and poorly paid operations and allow Rhodesian farmers to hire Mozambicans and Nyasalanders. Within South Africa itself there was a clear hierarchy as well. South Africans generally succeeded in evading the mines, whose workforce depended on migrants from outside the Union, preferring to find their own way to the cities where the best wages and freest conditions could be found.

The majority of African miners on the gold mines of the Witwatersand were from southern Mozambique until the era of the Great Depression. In the 1930s, the recruiters were allowed to bring in large numbers of migrants from Nyasaland (Malawi) while Basutoland (Lesotho) became progressively more and more important as a source of labour. Workforces from these three sources were balanced with smaller groups from elsewhere for the next forty years. After independence, far fewer workers were recruited from Mozambique while the Malawian government withdrew recruitment facilities and restricted migration. At the same time, in the 1970s the proportion of workers coming from South Africa increased dramatically (requiring a considerable hike in real wages), although most of them actually were drawn from the purportedly independent states such as Transkei and Ciskei, from which access to the South African urban labour market was becoming extremely difficult.

Although the migrant workers, especially the miners of

the southern part of the continent, are perhaps the best-known, in fact other major migrant circuits flourished during the colonial era. Within Tanganyika, the sisal plantations relied on a large migrant labour force from the central and western parts of the colony, poorly served by transport and lacking a cash-crop base. From the Belgian territory of Ruanda-Urundi, large numbers of workers trekked to Uganda to work in the cotton, and later coffee, farms of African cash-crop farmers in the so-called Fertile Crescent. In West Africa, migrants came down from the savanna region to the coastal colonies to plant or harvest groundnuts, cocoa and work in the British run underground mines of the Gold Coast.

Whole armies of migrants were required to produce the cotton of the Sudanese Gezira, tropical Africa's largest exporting colony. According to Jay O'Brien

The colonial regime mobilised all its powers to meet the large demand for wage labour in the Gezira Scheme. With the regime securely entrenched and the countryside 'pacified', taxes were raised and more rigorously collected. The time of rural tax collection in key labour supply provinces was shifted from the end of the dry season . . . to the beginning of the cotton picking season . . . in order to ensure that peasants and pastoralists were relieved of their cash at the most opportune time. The regime aggressively pushed the marketing of Manchester cotton goods, tea, coffee and sugar into new areas and vigilantly monitored their sale and manipulated their supply and price in relation to local crop yields and grain and livestock prices. In times of critical labour shortage (e.g. 1942/1943 cotton harvest) they stopped supplies of consumer goods to rural districts and channeled them through the administrative offices of the Gezira Scheme. Traditional handicraft production came under direct assault, as when the British banned and then destroyed cotton cultivation (and thus independent cloth production) in provinces abutting the Gezira. (O'Brien, 1983, 19)

O'Brien points as well to the effective development of landlord–tenant relations that put migrating West Africans in the Sudan under obligation to work and into recruitment networks. Professional recruiters and the economic and other power relations into which they could tap were everywhere of great importance in creating the migrant labour forces. Finally, and related closely to this last point, it was far from coincidental that so many migrant source areas were dominated by African chiefs and equivalent authorities who were paid by colonial regimes to help build up the number of workers.

From the nineteenth century even before the era of colonialism, the growing groundnut export crop of Senegambia relied on what were known in Gambia as 'strange farmers' who came from the interior and planted and harvested the crop in employment to landowners. In Senegal, such men became known as *navétanes*, a word which referred to their seasonal comings in the Sudanese winter. The *navétanes* were instrumental to the expansion of this major African export crop. While they were wage labourers, however, it is difficult to class them as proletarians. They established relations with their employers that used some of the language and forms of pre-capitalist clientage and slavery relationships (although the *navétanes* were entirely free before the law). The employer functioned as a host or landlord and the migrant workers often had the right to his food or the cultivation of a patch of his land. There was the possibility of the *navétane* settling down permanently in this situation but only were he to be given land of his own. Otherwise he retained his roots back in what is today Mali or Guinea.

Peter Waterman's detailed study of the Lagos docks suggests that here too what seems at first sight to be a proletarian workforce actually consisted of migrant workers who retained strong linkages to areas of origin and who related to work in terms of patronage ties that were crucial in securing jobs and establishing the way jobs were per-

formed. Dock workers have historically been casual workers in most ports until relatively recently and because of the
seasonal and completely variable nature of ship arrivals,
capital long resisted any attempt to decasualise such work.
Fred Cooper, in considering the dock workers of Mombasa,
has however insisted that for a long phase, casual hiring
contained advantages for peasant workers, assuring them
of a certain level of independence from employers and
enabling wage labour to be but one string on their bow.

In general, the social structures supporting migrant
labour in twentieth-century Africa have been the site for a
complex class struggle. Depending on the conjuncture of
social and economic forces, migrancy could benefit categories of workers given the possibilities open to them or it could
be used as a powerful weapon against the workers. East
African scholars have demonstrated repeatedly that migrant workers were able, when they strategised effectively,
to be quite successful in parlaying small sums of saved cash
into entrepreneurial possibilities. In Kenya, the 'kulaks' of
today are typically descended from the most successful
migrants, those who secured a reasonable mix of conditions
and pay and who had wives or other dependents working
their fields for them at the same time. A study of rural
society in the Western Usambara mountains of Tanzania
has also insisted on the centrality of migrants to the formation of the most prosperous layer of the peasantry (Sender,
1974). At the same time, migration at a stress point in one's
life cycle, pushing one into a job offering little, fed into
circumstances that were harsh, oppressive and destructive
of life.

To outward appearances, what was operating was a dual
economy, a market economy in which labour participated
as wage workers and a subsistence economy, based on the
direct realisation of use value, that is to say where people
could gain their livelihood out of unmarketed resources to

which they had access. An important school of writers has emphasised that these sectors were 'articulated' through the colonial economy which required both elements to function efficiently. The colonial state actually tried to keep some areas as zones that yielded only workers who had to migrate to earn money, while the local authorities profited from the migration system. Regional differences in economic development can partly be blamed on this strategy.

Until World War II, this was the dominant aspect of wage labour in colonial Africa – mining and agriculture attracted what capital entered, workers tended to be unskilled migrants. Some have found it convenient to write about 'colonial capitalism' defined in this way. The 1940s, however, witnessed an important increase in the weight and numbers of wage workers in African economies. The war cut Africa off from Europe creating the possibility for unprecedented industrial development while war demands re-imposed conscripted labour on African cultivators. While jobs were available and wage rates rose, inflation intensified the need for more and more cash in most regions.

These forces not only created a new African proletariat in quantitative terms but made that proletariat into a militant collectivity as measured by united action enabling us to talk about the existence of a *class*. The end of World War II and the years following saw strike action of colony-wide importance, including general strikes, in many parts of the continent. What made such activities as the East African port strikes of 1947–48 (affecting Zanzibar, Dar es Salaam and Mombasa), the railway workers' struggle in French West Africa at the same time and the national strike of Nigerian workers in 1945 so effective and threatening to colonial regimes was their concentration among workers in the transport and communication sectors essential to the colonial economies. In the history of strikes and collective resistance on the part of workers throughout Africa, it is remarkable how the same occupational groupings recur again and again. Dock workers, railway workers especially, and also postal and telegraph workers, were the pioneers of unionisation and the spread of socialist ideas in Africa. They had a territory-wide consciousness which contrasted with the more parochial loyalties of those more bound to older loyalties and a strategic significance that completely outweighed their numerical modesty.

They included within their numbers an important group of skilled workers who had a consequent relation to work somewhat unlike that of the general labourer. Skilled workers were rare and in heavy demand in early colonial Africa. In southern Africa, skilled labour was most frequently white labour although even here, the mines were a focus for African men with skills (Moroney in Marks and Rathbone, 1982). Immigrants from India were the artisans of the new East African towns. In West Africa, the situation was different. By the nineteenth century, Africans in the coastal ports had acquired, through commercial habituation, travel and mission training, the typical skills of European manufacture and brought them into the interior in the wake of imperial conquest. In Northern Nigeria, skilled workers typically earned five or six times what an unskilled labourer could make, a figure not out of line with equivalent 'racist' ratios in the southern part of the continent. However, these figures were watered down and wages became less satisfactory. By the 1940s, skilled workers were feeling the pinch through inflation and prepared to act in conjunction with general labourers – an explosive combination.

A special category of skilled worker was the clerk. African white-collar workers were essential to the functioning of the colonial bureaucracies. They included both officials who were essentially managers and lower-level workers who were very much employees, despite the felt distance between themselves and the masses. State workers, including teachers, were another important component in the growing salience of organised labour in the decade following World War II in much of Africa. According to Sharon Stichter, perhaps 2–3 per cent of African wage workers in Kenya in 1947 were clerks and another 7 per cent artisans (Sandbrook and Cohen, 1975, 38). This proportion was small; the continued numerical dominance of the unskilled and the strategic role of the skilled were two central components in the mixture within the African working population.

Post-war development strategies involved attempts to generalise commodity production further in Africa. By the mid 1950s, Thomas Hodgkin guessed that there were four to five million wage workers in tropical colonial Africa. Proportionately they ranged from 24 per cent of the total population of Southern Rhodesia, where capitalist production was very firmly planted, to 1.5 per cent of the total population of Nigeria, among the more substantial territories (Hodgkin, 1956, 118).

Ralph Grillo made a detailed study of railway workers in Uganda some years after independence which exemplifies some of these points (Grillo, 1973, 1974). One feature which distinguished Ugandan railway workers in general was the sense of community that they shared, partially derived from the workplace with its characteristic hierarchy of skill and status and particular forms of communication and partially from the separate railway housing in which they lived apart from the Ugandan population at large. The railway workers learnt to adapt easily to life in another town or indeed, until independence, to another East African territory. Their lives were much the same in Mombasa or Dar es Salaam as in Kampala. They possessed a broad range of job-related skills and a commitment to railway work that was likely to last through a man's life. Such workers formed only a small minority of the urban workforce in Uganda, which itself has always had a rather small percentage of city dwellers or wage workers in the total population but it is easy to see why they deserve the strategic attention that researchers, politicians and administrations have given to them.

By the 1940s, thanks to the growing intensity of the cash nexus and the unfavourable circumstances for procuring cash in much of the countryside, one can talk more generally about a growing town population cut off from rural economic life. When the Great Depression hit the copper mines of south-central Africa at the beginning of the 1930s, the population of the new towns in Northern Rhodesia as well as the established settlements in Katanga (Belgian Congo) east of the frontier shrank drastically; most of the workforce drifted back to the land. However with the copper boom that immediately preceded World War II, African families settled in the mining zone in large numbers and established a commitment to urban life and mine labour that has to be considered apart from the economic issue of wages alone. Urban growth in Africa proceeded rapidly during World War II and has not ceased to advance steadily since. Let us take an extreme example. Leopoldville, capital of the Belgian Congo, held 26,000 inhabitants in 1935. This figure surpassed 100,000 by the end of the war, reached perhaps 400,000 at independence in 1960 and today estimates for Kinshasa range upwards from 2,000,000.

With the cut-off from Europe, African secondary industry was able to develop in a number of centres. A large enough market existed for a few basic consumer goods, such as cooking oil, cigarettes, beer, and soft drinks to be manufactured in the bigger and more urbanised African colonies. The range of items that could be made locally on a profitable basis was much greater in those colonies with a substantial settler population and it was in Bulawayo and Salisbury in Southern Rhodesia, in Dakar and Leopoldville, Nairobi and the capitals of the Portuguese colonies that a bigger range of factories producing consumer goods came to life. By contrast to the situation before the war, colonial governments came themselves to favour local industrialisation that served colonial markets and encouraged metropolitan investments and even exports of intermediate goods. With the coming of independence, tariffs and other measures were instituted to forward this kind of development more substantially.

In economic terms, the results of this policy of industrialisation are arguably rather mixed. Many of the industries established produce goods of inferior quality that depend heavily on imported inputs to operate. Only in a couple of countries (Zimbabwe, Nigeria) has even a limited capital goods sector emerged. Africa has shown little capacity at exporting manufactured goods. However, a material basis exists for the rise of a small class of industrial workers in the bigger urban centres. In up to two dozen tropical African cities, it is now possible to identify neighbourhoods where the population is predominantly dependent on industrial labour and must follow the rhythms of industrial time and industrial discipline at the workplace. Such centres include a higher proportion of workers with skills.

The situation of this industrial working class, however, is not quite the same as that of its comperes in the west. Within the fast-growing cities, it forms a small minority compared to the larger number of employees outside industry and the many people who make a living entirely outside regularised wage employment. Nationally, wage labour is still a component in a larger economy that is weighted towards the rural and towards the production of value outside the structures of capitalism. This point is particularly worth emphasising because of the difficult situation in which African economies have largely been placed in the 1980s.

The early independence years were relatively favourable to the expansion of industries set up in response to tariff barriers against imports and other state devices to boost 'development'. In Tanzania, wage employment in manufacturing rose from 23,583 in 1964 to 64,921 in 1974, at almost the pace of increased value added (Coulson in Fransman, 1982, 69). However, growing national indebtedness, negative balances of payment and infrastructural decline have led to this process being halted or even reversed. This is true in the self-consciously socialist states putting emphasis on industry as much or more than the others.

In Tanzania, for instance, coupled with the expansion of industrial employment, state service work has also grown markedly since independence. However, the largest single source of wage labour, the sisal plantations, shed workers in the 1960s as the international market for sisal declined and on such a scale that the total number of Tanzanians working for a wage hardly grew in absolute numbers and actually declined as a proportion of the total. This is a common story throughout Africa. Only in a few cases, most strikingly Nigeria in the wake of the oil boom after 1973, has there been a large increase in the number of jobs created. In Nigeria, this increase had little directly to do with the oil industry which employs very few workers. It came instead through the dramatic expansion in the service sector, in state employment and the provision of consumer goods for the greatly increased civil service.

Generally speaking, the classic processes of proletarianisation outlined by Marx are occurring in rural Africa but Africans do not confront a powerful or effective indigenously based capitalism anxious to make use of their labour. The problem is compounded by the decay of rural production in many countries. Feeder zones for migrant labour now no longer have viable subsistence bases that operate effectively.

In recent years, Johan Pottier returned to Mambwe country in Zambia where Watson had done his classic work on the impact of migrant labour on the Copper Belt in the

1950s. Today, on the one hand, the capacity of the peasantry to reproduce their way of life relatively autonomously has diminished very significantly while on the other, the opportunities for migrants in cities in Zambia are few. Zambia is the extreme case in Africa where the development of copper mining has led to virtually half the entire population living in urban areas (and absolute declines in rural populations in many districts). However, the economic basis for urbanisation other than the mines and the operations of the Zambian state is thin and agricultural production has suffered severely from the loss of people and resources. In fact, the migration to the cities has fallen off with the decay in the economy from the 1970s. The problem cannot be understood entirely from its urban dimension, however. Jay O'Brien suggests that from the 1970s, Sudanese agricultural labour has become subject to a generalised national labour market reflecting the breakdown of a coherent peasant or pastoral core economy relatively independent of cash needs and thus to the breakdown of the neat articulation, so typical of colonial Africa, between the cash and 'traditional' economies. (O'Brien, 1983). This breakdown of the barrier between town and countryside is well-observed for South Africa, where similarly there is no real expansion of urban jobs to accommodate the desperate need for cash to survive.

At the same time, with the prospects of viability in the countryside weakening, there is a large population in Africa that is urbanised and job-seeking. It faces all the basic material problems of workers in more industrialised countries: seeking food, shelter and necessities as well as the possibilities for familial reproduction in the urban environment. Thus, Jim Silver writes about Ghanaian gold miners that

the mines work force had become, relative to earlier years, a highly stabilized social category. Workers now bring their families to the mines and stay for years, acquiring training and skills in mining, and making it their life's work. Furthermore, the social category is reproducing itself, as evidenced by the growing numbers of second generation mineworkers, especially amongst the previously most migratory northerners. (83, ROAPE 12, 1978)

Women in Africa no longer fall outside the typical working categories; they are also defining themselves as individuals in search of cash and a wage. Materially, conditions for wage workers vary. Some commanding relatively scarce skills might be said to constitute a labour aristocracy but the majority are poor men and women who survive on narrow margins. As educational skills so rare in colonial times become more generalised while economic opportunities fail to expand, the protective armour of 'labour aristocrats' has become in any case rapidly less effective in most instances. The African wage worker lives in a tight nexus of rising costs and declining services that determine material life for an individual or a family.

❧ 3 ❧

CULTURE, COMMUNITY AND CLASS

In the previous chapter, we established the material basis for the existence and development of a working class in contemporary Africa. It is really this notion of class that makes so much of the relevant literature of the past ten to fifteen years seem fresh and interesting. The idea of class brings Africa into living connection with the circumstances of workers in other parts of the world and in discussions about politics and society on an international basis. Two aspects of the idea of class are particularly relevant here. First, there is the concept of a proletariat inherently antagonistic to those who command labour-power and to the capitalist system that they organise and drive forward. In 1848, Karl Marx and Friedrich Engels wrote that all genuinely proletarian politics aimed at

the formation of the proletariat into a class; the overthrow of the bourgeois supremacy; and the conquest of political power by the proletariat. The theoretical conclusions of the Communists are in no way based on ideas or principles that have been invented or discovered by this or that would-be universal reformer. They merely express, in general terms, actual relations springing from an existing class struggle, from a historical movement going on under our very eyes. (Marx and Engels, *The Communist Manifesto*, 25–26)

This powerful analysis assumes that through its formation and development, the working class must pursue a particular kind of politics centred on its existence as a class. A 'revisionist' or modified form of class determination of history is supported as well by those who reject the assumption that working-class politics must take a revolutionary form.

Secondly, a substantial literature assumes, quite apart from the political ramifications, that the working class is a bounded society linked to specific community structures and constituting a distinct cultural entity that may both resist or adapt to capitalist values and structures. In the most important work of Marxist historiography of our time, Edward Thompson's *The Making of the English Working Class*, the author forthrightly excuses his exclusion of Scotland and Wales from his discussion by pointing out that 'class is a cultural as much as an economic formation' (Thompson, 1963, 13).

Africanists, uncomfortable with the notion of class, have tended to dismiss such approaches as irrelevant because they come from outside the continent. In his writings on African socialism, for instance, former President Julius Nyerere of Tanzania is insistent that class is a Eurocentric and morally undesirable intrusion both conceptually and to the extent that any such phenomenon has actually won a foothold in Africa. Yet scholars have uncovered a culturally and politically distinct working class in such extra-European cities as Lima and Shanghai and class-centred politics has been a major force in numerous countries of Asia and Latin America, if far less consistently than in Europe. In Africa, the evidence for class behaviour, culturally and politically, (as opposed to manifest inequalities) is more ambiguous but it will not do to explain this limitation in terms of some kind of essential Africanness. It is crucial to understand how class does work in the African context, though, because otherwise we are left with inoperative 'universal' definitions or we are back to a limited and purely eclectic understanding of workers as individuals gathered in a workplace or slum.

During the colonial era, class conflict in African colonies was largely relegated, in the eyes of writers who sympathised with anti-colonial movements, to a subordinate feature of the colonial and racial structure of society. Thus when Terence Ranger wrote an assessment of *beni* dancing, a major urban art-form, widely spread through eastern and central Africa in the first half of the twentieth century, he sensitively explored how the dance themes and structures brought out a relationship to the values and power polarities of colonialism, and commented on them. Despite the special attraction for urban workers of the dance societies, he chose to stress colonialism rather than class in his approach (Ranger, 1975). Many studies have noted that colonial workers understood conflict and oppression in terms of racism or the conquest of their country by an overweening crowd of foreigners rather than along lines of property ownership or as a consequence of any natural antagonism between classes. Yet, as has been pointed out earlier, the advance of the nationalist movement did not mean that organised workers' movements simply joined in an uncomplicated manner. On the contrary, in most African colonies increasing antagonisms developed as the newly empowered nationalist parties attempted to formulate labour policies and to eliminate power bases in society that lay beyond their control. It is this which leads one to propose the propriety of exploring a particular working class *consciousness* in African social and political life. One can start to examine African workers as a class first by examining the workplace itself. The sociologist Michael Burawoy, who has studied mining in Zambia in comparison with work situations in very different societies, refers to the 'politics of production' (Burawoy, 1985). He points to the need to investigate seriously, rather than to assume, the nature of authority on the job, attempts to mould a cultural and political hegemony by employer and state as well as the way workers inter-relate. In Zambia, he was most struck by the arbitrary and colonial nature of authority as it prevailed before independence. The legitimation of the employer was the legitimation of the conqueror. During the colonial period, if blacks were dependent children to supervisors, the black workers perceived the bosses and supervisors essentially as whites who colluded to put the Zambian in his place and to exploit him in a context with proportionately more white workers than on the South African gold mines. This was one touchstone for some fierce workplace struggles between 1935 and independence in 1964. The old type of authority, however, has given ground over the last twenty years with Zambianisation. The Zambian worker at present has become subject to Zambian supervision while the copper companies are nationalised. According to Burawoy, *no* effective system of control has effectively been instituted to replace the old one. Even the significant number of remaining white employees do not behave in the old way towards Africans while the new Zambian hierarchy, although committed to a management ideology, has lost much of the effective power over the workplace that its white predecessors enjoyed (Burawoy, 1972). This is not unrelated to the decline in the copper industry under the weight of poor world prices in the broader setting.

Given their scale and remarkable social organisation, it is hardly surprising that relatively so much research has been done on the mines of southern Africa. There are now several careful studies of the labour process on these mines which enables us to talk with some authority about questions of authority, solidarity, dignity and survival in this dangerous and difficult work environment. Some of the work on mines emphasises the authoritarian character of the system with little reserve. Thus Bruce Fetter has described the colonial regime of the Union Minière du Haut-Katanga, so closely linked to that of the Belgian state and the Catholic Church, as *totalitarian* (Fetter, 1973). This is not entirely sufficient in explaining how the work structure actually is experienced by men, although it certainly is the right term for what the tripartite system (state–church–company) intended.

Rob Gordon has investigated human interaction in a Namibian mine compound (Gordon, 1977). He has established the importance of the ties that men establish between themselves and their 'brothers', as they call them, at work, and the intense network of money-producing services and side-activities that motivate the men in the compound. Relationships between white supervisors and African miners are distant in that Africans are careful to try to keep their thoughts to themselves and do what they can to organise work in ways that seem most safe and reasonable for their own interests. However, whites and blacks also form unequal clientage relationships which tie closely into the informal and illegal aspects of the compound economy.

Dunbar Moodie's study of the South African gold mines relates well to that of Gordon. An important part of Moodie's emphasis lies in discerning the way that a large and important stratum of black intermediaries who sit between the small number of white supervisors and managers and the mine-face workers actually function. While mine rules largely determine formal behaviour in terms ultimately based on corporate profitability, the black worker actually negotiates informally with the black supervisor about the permitted scope of a range of illegal and semi-legal activities. Moodie has penetrated the world of homosexuality in the compounds and considers other illicit activities where access to power and services indicates a fairly complex authority pattern (Moodie, 1983). He takes the sum of worker behaviour at the mines as being 'mine culture'. He looks at aspects of this culture such as money, migration, sex, safety and race, but not directly at class formation, however, just like Gordon. As a result, despite the richness of his portrayal, he has difficulty explaining what actually goes on in the mine except in personal and psychological terms. The situational context which Moodie and Gordon both derive in large part from the American student of 'deference and demeanour', Erving Goffman, is too readily interchangeable with any other non-work context in which unequal power relationships prevail.

It is much easier to understand how the gold mines operate in class terms in South Africa now that the miners are beginning successfully to organise themselves into a trade union, the National Union of Mineworkers. NUM has recently sponsored a study of safety in the gold mines which is largely concerned to dispel the idea that the white supervisory workers are fundamental to the working of good safety procedures (Leger, 1985). Instead, their role has become more and more nakedly that of enhancing productivity and increasing the workload. While Gordon accepts that the mineowner in Namibia has been anxious to keep a racial and ethnic mix that reflects the social hierarchy in force outside the mine, Leger, in his NUM report, sees this racial hierarchy on the outside as serving purposes of control within the mine world. Research into the labour process of this kind can be a very rich source of information on the inter-relation of work with authority, control, co-operative and patrimonial human relations, and the whole question of class in the broader society.

One early attempt to re-formulate ideas about the African working class that had an important impact was made by Giovanni Arrighi and John Saul who spoke about a division between two kinds of workers (1973, also Arrighi, 1970). The majority are essentially unskilled rural migrants whose political roots and cultural values lie largely in the countryside and who are most comfortable with a populist nationalist position. By contrast, there is also a small stratum of skilled, effectively urbanised and fully proletarianised African workers who tend to be found in the employ of the state or big multi-national corporations. They are relatively few in number, well-paid, well-organised and often impervious to nationalist influence which they might actually even find a threat to their material interests. Hence they formed a sort of labour aristocracy. Much of the literature of the past decade actually began as a critique of and reaction to the labour aristocracy hypothesis which must now have rather few defenders in the pure form. Yet in one way, the current investigator can still particularly benefit from the Arrighi–Saul approach. It pointed early to investigating different layers of the African working class which actually can have very different cultural and political approaches to society.

Richard Jeffries was the author of one of the earliest and most telling critiques of the labour aristocracy thesis based on fieldwork in the cities of Sekondi and Takoradi which developed in the colonial Gold Coast as the site of an important harbour and railway terminus. Jeffries sees this complex, the third largest urban agglomeration in Ghana, as dominated by an employed, relatively skilled working class rather than the typical situation where the working class is merely a small fraction within a broader social fabric. Far from being an isolated and passive labour aristocracy, the organised workers constitute a politically cohesive elite that 'the common people of Sekondi–Takoradi came to look to . . . to express a generalised sense of exploitation and social justice' (Jeffries, 1975, 69). The golden era when this relationship was most sharply and organically expressed came in the days of Nkrumah, when the harbour and railway workers mounted dramatic if ultimately unsuccessful opposition against the national regime, which was seen as the corrupt instrument of a distant ruling class in the capital. The general strike of 1961 brought the workers of Sekondi–Takoradi out very effectively. The skilled workers have always been better off than the average labourer but they distinguish themselves in terms of income, living standard and social outlook more sharply from the white-collar world because it appears to live off them parasitically. Between themselves and the national 'elite', Jeffries would argue for the importance of a boundary of considerably greater significance than that amongst workers.

Another British social scientist, Jeff Crisp, has investigated the history of a different segment of the Ghanaian working class, the gold miners (Crisp, 1984). The miners, in his account, similarly feel a common sense of oppression based on the experience of harsh work conditions, of the living facilities available in what are in essence company towns and on the gulf that exists between themselves and the management. This is true despite the considerable differentiation of skill level and salary among the workers. "In such an environment it has not been difficult for the 'adamant radicals' of the labour force, the skilled and experienced underground workers, to mobilize their colleagues" (Crisp, 1984, 182). The miners have a long history of resistance and militancy to management and the state and knowledge of this history is readily passed on through generations of workers.

However, it is very striking to observe as well that the Ghanaian gold miners have never shown an interest in forming a working-class political party nor have they been interested in relating to the left nationalism which forms an important part of the intellectual baggage of the Ghanaian petty bourgeoisie. Contrary to Arrighi and Saul, the poorly-paid, illiterate underground workers do not relate to the outlook of nationalist politicians at all. Their struggles hover close to the workplace and Crisp actually does not see them as class-conscious in so far as class-consciousness implies a capacity to relate to the struggles of other workers in the country. Nor are the railwaymen of Sekondi–Takoradi entirely different. They have an apparently clearer sense of themselves as spokesmen for the urban poor and a more definite vision of their place *vis-à-vis* national politics. However, they have never found a comfortable relation with the radical intelligentsia either in or out of power in the state nor have they seen the purpose of establishing a workers' or socialist party as an alternative to the kind of politics that has typified Ghana. Antagonistic relations with Nkrumah's CPP probably tended to alienate them from socialism as a coherent ideology. In short, the world that is evoked by Jeffries and Crisp is one which is bounded and class-conscious in important ways but seems somewhat isolated in a wider society and unable to constitute a coherent basis for a class-based politics.

Jim Silver has also contributed to the study of Ghana's gold miners. He is more pessimistic about class unity than Crisp. He sees much more antagonism between the skilled surface workers, whose skills and connexions have generally allowed them to dominate the union and who relate better to national politics and the world of the new Ghanaian ruling class, and the underground workers, who come from the most backward part of Ghana, the north, which only has a small share in the process of formation of that ruling class. The alienation and suspicion that northerners feel about the national entity of Ghana helps to isolate them from a potential movement of national liberation or change (Silver, 1978 and 1981).

Perhaps, following Thompson, it must be conceded that specific cultural and political traditions themselves are fundamental in shaping the way a particular working class behaves. In most of West Africa, it is the coastal cities that have experienced the most industrialisation and economic development. In Nigeria, however, the main *entrepôt* of the savanna region, Kano, has grown into an important industrial centre. Paul Lubeck has researched its new working class and emphasises that the political life and workplace politics of the Kano worker is shaped in terms of Islamic Hausa culture (Lubeck, 1978). On the one hand, so long as a local employer can manipulate the symbols of that culture effectively, it may be difficult for workers to find a rationale or to organise on the basis of class. Indeed, many of the first factory organisers in Kano were Southerners. However, Lubeck appears to think that resistance based on a language validated through Islam is able to forge a different sort of consciousness in time. In other words, class formation has become distinctively meaningful but only as integrated into a culture very unlike that in which industrialisation originated historically in Europe. Islamic culture bears a flexibility and possibility for expressing social contradictions often ignored or stereotyped by outsiders. Islam contains within it a concept of secular oppression, of injustice and of community solidarity.

Once again using a West African model, it may be interesting to draw these themes together by considering the work of Adrian Peace on the factory workers of Ikeja on the Lagos mainland (Peace, 1979). Following independence in 1960, Ikeja became an important site for factories producing goods in response to Nigerian protectionist legislation for the Nigerian consumer market. It attracted a growing community of rural migrants, mainly young males at first, seeking factory work. In some respects, Peace confirms the ideas of Crisp and Jeffries for the workers that he has studied. As factory life has established itself in Ikeja, workers have gradually improved their capacity to organise and their involvement in militant activity. Life in the vicinity of Lagos reveals only too well the ostentation of the Nigerian rich and is vivid in the minds of the workers. Peace feels able to speak about a culture of resistance and a deep sense of awareness by the workers of the gulf that separates the management of the factories, who make the decisions, and themselves. In these ways, there is an important consciousness of class that builds very directly around the workplace.

However, Ikeja workers at the same time are part of a cultural milieu that they do not dominate in contrast to the Ghanaian communities mentioned. Nor is Peace convinced that the milieu is a very fertile one for the establishment either of a bounded working-class culture or a distinctive working-class politics. The typical Ikeja worker returns home to Agege, an old *entrepôt* community and railway terminus, where salaried men and women form very much of a minority. The dominant form of activity in Agege is self-employed work with an immense commercial sector so typical of urban Nigerian life. It is most likely that the workers' relatives or wives will themselves be engaged in the marketplace. So will the members of the networks, whether kinsmen, friends from the hometown, helpful elders, or 'brother'–neighbours – which are more important to him than the relations established at the workplace on the whole.

In general, being part of Agege also implies respect for and interaction with a crucial minority of landlords, trading entrepreneurs and other relatively wealthy people who live within the community and help to channel its cultural structures. Their importance militates decisively against a class-conscious politics succeeding outside the narrow industrial sphere. Moreover, the industrial worker continues to aspire very intensely himself towards self-employment, which has vastly more prestige than wage labour in Yoruba culture. In the classic approach to proletarianisation of Marx, workers are supposed to learn from their common work pride in a better and more knowledgeable means of organising society. Peace's workers, however, fight proletarianisation and are ashamed of proletarian identification. They aspire to be their own men and women. The highly skilled are precisely those most apt to succeed in establishing some kind of business on the side. The other workers identify strongly with their successes and with a business approach to life generally even though the actual chances of breaking away from the factory entirely are clearly mediocre for the whole workforce.

Agege is not untypical of African urban environments in its mixture of an incoherent mass of poor people involved in a myriad of activities together with an influential small stratum of power-broking entrepreneurs. In Nairobi, Janet Bujra sees such individuals as promoting a vague populist ethos that defends their own interests while apparently hitting out at the problem of poverty and the situation of the poor. They become effective patrons (Bujra, 1978–79). Michael Chege believes that the 'crowd' of poor Nairobi men and women shifted from the anti-colonial focus of the 1940s and 1950s to operating as supporters or opponents of protagonists in Kenyan elections. He has produced a study of Bujra's power-brokers as they actually operate in general elections in the poorest parts of Nairobi. In Dagoretti and Mathare Valley constituencies, 'we found small, proper-tied, powerfully organized groups swaying the political inclinations of large segments of the urban crowd against their opponents, particularly where the material objectives of the latter can be somehow identified with the former' (Chege, 1981).

Returning again to Nigeria, Peter Waterman has taken related material and considered Nigerian workers' atti-tudes, as uncovered in surveys, as 'conservative'. The work-ers he polled admired the rich and successful while hoping that these might function responsibly as patrons. They placed considerable weight on an ethos whereby each indi-vidual attempts to set himself or herself up in commerce or other petty business activity. This conservatism he relates, not to the values that prevail in contemporary conservative

Western circles, but to those that prevail among non-wage workers in Nigerian towns and among the rural population; they have a traditional character that links back to pre-colonial ideology (Waterman, 1976). In certain defensive kinds of confrontations, 'conservatives', or rather workers bearing conservative values, in fact act in very militant ways against capitalism. Nigeria is a particularly important test case for working-class culture and politics in Africa because of the overall size of the wage-earning population and because the weakness of socialist politics has always been coupled with militant industrial action and even historic waves of general strikes (1945, 1964, 1971, 1975, 1981).

What tends to come forth from the work of writers such as Waterman, Jeffries, Bujra, Chege and others is that the typical politics of African workers is most easily encompassed as 'populist'. African populism is potentially conservative in the cultural forms it takes and the set of beliefs to which it adheres, as Waterman or Lubeck show. However, it is radical when set against the advance of the new African ruling class now stripped of whatever aura of promise it held before independence. This class is not often defined primarily in terms of ownership of the means of production; what it has in common, as a means of accumulating wealth and reproducing that process of accumulation, is access to state power and office. Thus the 'elite' is typically linked to Western life-styles and to educational prowess. It consists of the rich, the Big Men, the Wa Benzi who drive around in Mercedes cars. The class antagonisms aimed at these post-colonial inheritors are intense. African fiction such as the work of the Ghanaian Armah, the Nigerian Iyayi or the Kenyan Meja Mwangi bear witness to the way this populism is constructed. Because it lacks a clear perspective however, a materially vague populism is unlikely to be a means out of underdevelopment and chaotic living conditions for the poor. It contains little interpretation of the production process and is fairly easily manipulable even though it bursts forth in waves of rage at the existing authorities from time to time and has helped to topple governments.

Such emotions first were obvious in the decade after World War II, accompanied by the great surge of urbanisation as men and women were displaced by capitalism in unprecedented numbers. Frank Furedi, writing about Kenya on the eve of Mau Mau, characterised the Nairobi poor as an urban 'crowd' rather like those that were part of the revolutionary processes of the eighteenth and early nineteenth centuries in Europe (Furedi, 1973). The intensity of struggle and the violence of resistance to capital and the state in this period often bore witness to the low level of integration of workers in an urban life or to collective forms of protest typical of an industrial society. Instead, what historians have noticed is the early and quite complex form of resistance to capital at the workplace and outside whose ferocity and success played an important blocking role in the early history of capitalist enterprise in Africa. Their effort has recovered the pre-history of the African worker.

Perhaps the richest example lies in van Onselen's pioneering study of Rhodesian gold mines in the first third of the twentieth century (van Onselen, 1976). Van Onselen is concerned to destroy the myth of the passive African who was not permitted to function as a serious social and historical character on the stage of industrial life by past writers closer to a colonial outlook. The migrant workers to the Rhodesian gold fields in van Onselen's study are involved in a large range of activities that he considers to be resistant to capital, including desertion, slacking and destruction of tools, disguised forms of strikes (as well as some actual ones) and shrewd ability to operate between different employers. In a book co-authored with Ian Phimister, van Onselen suggests that 'from the very earliest years of capital-intensive industry Africans had a well developed and demonstrable self-awareness of their position as exploited workers' which can be assessed through 'worker strategy in the context of the overall functioning of the political economy and in day-to-day responses in the work situation' (Phimister and van Onselen, 1978, 2).

Others have generalised this kind of analysis into a consideration of 'worker consciousness'. Thus Robin Cohen contrasts overt and hidden forms of resistance consciousness among African workers. Hidden forms of resistance include desertion, community withdrawal from the colonial economy (typical mainly in early periods of control), the preference for target work, resistance to controls over the work process, sabotage, creation of a work culture with elements of resistance in it, the feigning of accidents and disease or their use as a means of resisting inhumane conditions, drug and alcohol use, the turning towards religious sects that sustain cultural independence and theft from employers (Cohen, 1980). Cohen sees hidden resistance as a kind of underground well of consciousness from which a stream of overt industrial or political activity appears from time to time in propitious circumstances. Jean Bonis, examining labour conflict in Mauritanian mines, highlights an elemental and utterly undisciplined working-class resistance that breaks up the work process when conditions appear intolerable and is mediated after a time through the union officials and others who can intervene in a lull between the storm of angry protest and the authorities at the right moment (Bonis, 1973).

Is there an historical progression from this kind of all-embracing resistance which constantly challenges aspects of the employers' order and the evolution of a more systematic and disciplined kind of resistance that we can more easily consider as class consciousness? Another historian of central Africa, Charles Perrings, uncovered considerable evidence of equivalent forms of 'worker consciousness' in the copper mines of Northern Rhodesia and the Belgian Congo from an early stage (Perrings, 1979). However, he is inclined to dismiss their significance until the point where the process of proletarianisation was developed enough for systematic strikes to be organised and for trade unions to evolve.

An interesting critique of van Onselen by Melvin Goldberg develops the point (Goldberg, 1981). The kind of resistance that is rife in the goldfields of early Rhodesia has an importance and an impact. It is in some respects strengthened precisely because of the rural linkages of the workers and the means by which they can withdraw their labour entirely from the market. However, Goldberg is insistent that this is different from what social science has meant by proletarianisation and it must be distinguished from the kind of activity that is characteristic of working-class activity developed from within a genuinely capitalist mode of production.

In another mining setting in Africa, the tin mines field of Northern Nigeria, a remarkable feature of worker response to capitalist mining activity has been the expansion of a market in stolen tin and the turning of entire communities towards tin theft as a major activity. This pattern became particularly extensive during the period when colonial rule began to wane and only intensified after independence. In a sense, tin theft is a form of resistance to capitalist (and, until recently, foreign) ownership of resources and instruments of labour and it is consciously understood as such by the communities involved. However, it is equally true that tin theft mainly lines the pockets of a locally based accumulating class in reality. It is not a form of resistance that can effectively bring a class of oppressed together and make them conscious of an alternative means of structuring society. Instead it points to the strength of petty commodity production in Nigeria and the success of this kind of economic structure where capitalism has only taken partial hold of society (Freund, 1982).

To survey the work that has been done on worker resistance and consciousness in tropical Africa is to encounter a wide range of experiences, some of which can be understood only in terms of a specific history. It is undoubtedly true that the bulk of wage labour has consisted of unskilled workers closely linked to the values of the village and a sense of community with deep pre-colonial roots. Such workers are not apt spontaneously to form working-class parties and they do not constitute a bounded class with a bounded class experience. However, this is not to say that they are incapable of a radical response to what in their terms represents intolerable conditions, treatment or pay and the response is one that does reflect a confrontation with the employer, with capital.

At the same time, the increasingly important community of workers with skills, committed to urban life and wage labour, is apt to make radical responses comparable to those of workers elsewhere in the world once we admit that they generally represent a minority of the poor in the setting in which they are living. Workers of this kind may appear to exhibit conservative patterns of political and social response too. The whole spectrum of African workers are in fact best understood as being capable of a range of political responses.

From the considerable studies of workers made in Africa in recent years, the following conclusions can perhaps be safely drawn. One is that the circumstances in which African workers live rarely encourage the formation of a distinct working class, proletarian identification as opposed to a general sense of identification with the poor and antagonism to those who have come to possess the keys to the kingdom of wealth and power in the new Africa. There is rather little sense of a rational political activity that would lead to a different form of the state or a state that would actively promote the interests of workers. The specific history of African nationalism and African 'socialism' with their hostility to independent worker organisation and their often successful appropriation of the language of social transformation for their own ends may be one explanation. Another is surely the objective circumstances in which African workers live: the relatively uneven penetration of capitalist social forms and ideas into most parts of Africa and the prevalence of economic activities other than wage-labour, especially wage-labour in manufacturing industry.

Having said this, it is wrong to conclude consequently that we had best forget about the worker in coming to grips with social issues in Africa. In fact, the worker does have a significant reality. The workplace and what happens at it does help to shape his or her consciousness to a major extent. Strike action, populist protests with a definite working-class edge, form an important part of political life in periods of crisis in Africa. There is in fact much more that we need to know about these questions in various sectors of African life. An American historian has recently written, commenting on the eternal search by left-wing American historians for why socialism failed to develop on American soil: 'The question posed by Sombart two generations ago should be turned on its head; rather than ask why there is no socialism in America, or no class consciousness in America, historians should find out more about the class perceptions that did exist' (Wilentz, 1983). Much the same needs to be said for the study of Africa historically and in the present.

4

WAGE LABOUR, NON-WAGE LABOUR AND THE TOTAL SPHERE OF PRODUCTION

Our whole understanding of the nature of work and the worker is shot through with one simple historical sequence: the peasant becoming a proletarian and that image is inevitably one of a man. Yet the African reality, while it does contain that sequence, historically and as part of the contemporary world, embraces a much wider frame. There are only a limited number of African workers who are employed in sizeable industrial firms and understood as workers in the statistics that the state puts out. A much larger number of people are engaged in labour, either working for themselves or for others, that does not appear at all in the so-called formal sector of the labour market. While such activities are generally associated with urban life, they are frequently linked to agrarian activity. Work on the land cannot simply be assimilated to an easily digested concept of the 'peasant'. Agricultural work itself needs to be subjected to an assessment if we wish to understand the wider context of the labour process and wage labour in Africa. Finally, the study of work in Africa cannot simply be limited to a view of what males do. To a very large extent, women's work in Africa is found outside the formal sphere of wage labour and it is of particular moment in agriculture so that it fits particularly well into the topical categories that will dominate this chapter.

Let us start with the issue of peasantry. Victor Allen, in a frequently cited article of 1972, took the position that the peasantry was the heart of the African working class. Considering the subjection to capital of cultivators in the form of migrant labour and other coercive and semi-coercive measures, on the one hand, and given the relative stability and prosperity of the waged industrial working class on the other, this seemed to be an arguable case for the peasant. Arrighi and Saul divided the African working class into two, of which the poorer and more militant part was defined in terms of its peasant roots and linkages (Arrighi and Saul, 1973). Such assessments echoed the view of African populist politicians. Thus in the Arusha Declaration, Julius Nyerere proclaimed that 'if we are not careful we might get to the position where the real exploitation in Tanzania is that of the town dwellers exploiting the peasants' (Nyerere, 1968, 243). Léopold Sédar Senghor, the Senegalese president, considered the peasantry to be the real working class of Senegal. Chief Gatsha Buthelezi, the chief minister of Kwa Zulu, the South African black 'homeland', likes to define his legitimacy in terms of a peasant youth which nonetheless seamlessly blends into an aristocratic heritage as well. Such generalised views of the peasantry are not only romantic and rather too conveniently ambiguous, they also serve to mask the realities of differentiation, of gender, of historical process and of the actual nature of labour in agriculture.

There is first of all the need to recognise the difference between the historic cultivator of pre-conquest Africa and the rural dweller of the colonial period and after, subject to a process that has been termed 'peasantisation' (Post, 1977). Peasantisation is a process by which cultivators increasingly separated the social division of labour and involvement in political processes from kinship obligations and structures, in which land ownership and use began to be more individuated, in which markets became central to production and a homogeneous and often very localised culture gave way to domination by an outside culture forged in the city by a distant ruling class. The dynamic of rural work, in other words, comes increasingly under the hands of outside forces which start to determine the outcome of that work, if not to determine how it proceeds on a daily basis. Can this process actually lead to the establishment of a stable, relatively undifferentiated 'peasant' class? Can it be mobilised into a class enemy of the capitalists – the opposite in effect of Marx's notorious view of the peasantry as a 'sack of potatoes' with little potential for unity or political clarity?

Many writers have placed analytical emphasis on dependency and the subjection of peasants to outside forces. One result is an association with the idea of the peasant population as lacking initiative, trapped into a cycle of decline and despair in which the only outlet can be flight to the city, if not overseas. The most extreme views of this type are often associated with the peasantries of southern Africa where harsh state legislation in the interests of various sectors of capital has enormously intensified dependency and immiseration. Colin Bundy's justly famous study of the peasantry of the eastern Cape Colony of South Africa in the nineteenth century offers a more cheerful view of the prospects open to his subjects during a critical historical phase when merchant interests were still predominant but he outlines an almost inexorable decline once the impact of mining capital and settler nationalism are effective (Bundy, 1979). Yet even here there has been a critique based on a harsher view of *internal* social forces in eastern Cape African society with a far more complex pattern of differentiation and class formation. According to Jack Lewis, the happy times for the peasantry were brief. The commoditised surplus produced by most rural households represented poverty and the exigencies of a colonial state rather than prosperity. Only a small if significant minority could take effective advantage of the links to the merchants (Jack Lewis, 1984).

The potential for a varied and complex agrarian response

in adjustment to outside pressure in much of tropical Africa existed and it has been suggested that it is an error to understand peasants only as the passive victims of pressures from the colonial state or capitalist interest (Ranger, 1978). In practice, they showed considerable capacity even in such colonies as Southern Rhodesia for finding ways of combining means of access to the increasingly essential cash so as to allow rural households to survive, if not to prosper. It has become fashionable in fact to emphasise the independence of the African peasantry to this day from any state authority in such a way as to form a serious block to economic development (Hyden, 1980).

If African peasantries are able to survive and bend to the general onslaught of capital, can we actually imagine a situation where capitalism can itself arise out of the conditions of agrarian production for a market? In order to do so, we must postulate either a successful capitalist estate development or the emergence of a class of prosperous farmers or rich peasants coupled with a corresponding proletarianisation of the workforce on the land. The former road was heavily favoured in the earlier phases of colonial rule in Africa which continued to the end to lend weight to metropolitan settlers and their attempts to create plantations based on large-scale land alienation.

The construction of a model capitalist plantation system on African soil was however not a simple matter. A number of writers on colonial African societies have tried to posit a plantation mode of production or generalised theory of the plantation, notably Roger van Zwanenberg writing about East Africa and Duncan Clarke analysing settler agriculture in Southern Rhodesia but there is in fact an enormous variation in the conditions on rural estates, too great to easily reconcile into a plantation model (van Zwanenberg, 1975 and Clarke, 1977a). In an important article that compares the sugar plantations of Natal (South Africa) with those of Queensland (Australia), Adrian Graves and Peter Richardson have rejected after consideration the idea that plantation systems are uniform in the way labour organisation operates on them. Compared to the classic West Indian plantation where 'sugar plantations developed upon the basis of the growing integration of economic functions of sugar production within the confines of the historic legacy of the domination of foreign capital, sugar plantations in South Africa and Australia developed in precisely the opposite direction' (Graves and Richardson, 1980, 225).

Settler planters had to struggle with the colonial state, with rival economic interests and, above all, with their prospective plantation labour force in order to operate effectively at all. The history of white settlement in the highlands of Kenya, for instance, was one of gradual encroachment onto the land, originally marked for whites only, where at first the colonists cultivated a very small proportion of the acreage that they staked out. They got relatively little labour out of a squatter population that was able to take advantage of the situation to create a relatively thriving and increasingly commercialised agriculture. It was only with the 1940s that excellent prices for tropical produce, such as coffee and tea, together with the economies offered by mechanisation and improved transport, gave to the settlers the upper hand and allowed them to plan the expulsion of many of the squatters and the retention of others only on condition that they become something more like a wage labour force (Furedi, 1976).

Where colonial regimes attempted to turn local aristocracies into improving landlords, as for instance, in the first years of British rule in Northern Nigeria, even greater difficulties ensued. The relation of those aristocrats to a certain kind of state, their dependence on slavery and their limited commitment to improved agrarian technology made them disappointing as imitators of the English landed gentry (Shenton, 1986). Frederick Cooper has in considerable depth explained how and why the plantation system of Zanzibar and its coastal possessions depended for its efficiency on a slave system which in turn was embedded in the specific social and ideological world of Islamic Swahili-speaking East Africa. The plantations did not really survive the end of slavery. Squatters effectively seized the land in coastal Kenya. On the island of Zanzibar the Arabised landowning class remained in control of their land titles but they did not really transform their former slaves into wage workers. Instead, those workers became squatters also who contributed to the clove harvest, but on terms not set by the landowner (Cooper, 1977, 1981a).

Generally speaking, the conditions that make for concentrated workforces under conditions of factory discipline prevail far less easily in agriculture than in industry. Once one gets beyond the primitive gang system that characterised American slave plantations, it is not easy to organise an effective system of labour control or discipline, particularly without the discipline that is finally provided by sophisticated machinery. The land, moreover, cannot be worked from nine to five each weekday of the year on an even rhythm. The weather and the measure of seasons intervene, drastically altering work needs from one point in the calendar to another. Economies of scale are often irrelevant. The small farmer, once he is unreservedly committed to market production, is typically far more productive on the land than the corporation unless such factory-like features as timber mills or sugar mills create a powerful counter-factor. For this reason, capitalism in agriculture has evolved differently than in industry even within 'industrialised' countries. Concentration of production and mechanisation has occurred but not to the point of monopolisation under the auspices of finance capital. The number of wage labourers in agriculture shows a tendency to decline relatively, if not absolutely, although there is renewed reliance on seasonal work aimed at the planting or harvest season.

These tendencies can be observed in agricultural trends in Africa particularly in the large-scale labour force on farms. In colonial Mozambique, the huge British-owned sugar estates came to rely on an elaborate hierarchy of labour containing significant numbers of artisans, a permanent core of resident manual workers and a floating population of migrants who came to the Zambesi valley in response to a variety of economic and political pressures (Vail and White, 1980). It has been very difficult for the socialist government of Mozambique to put together a viable system for large-scale sugar production matching its hunger for export earnings; pressure from workers on independence was towards a relaxation of discipline and a decline in production. By contrast, in socialist Algeria, on a former estate in the Mitidja south of Algiers studied by Claudine Chaulet, collective production survived under the new regime. Again a core labour force, now in theory involved in co-management but actually under firm bureaucratic state control, is supplemented by an impoverished force of migrant workers (Chaulet, 1971).

In Southern Rhodesia, the European farm system was held together by a virtually feudal system of legislation in the form of masters' and servants' ordinance structures. Even before the fall of the Smith regime, however, there was a growing evolution towards mechanisation, the introduction of a skilled labour force and the shedding of unskilled labour, in other words, the development of a more capitalist system of social relations. This has meant the decline of dependence on migrants from Malawi and Mozambique and a situation whereby increasing proportions of the labour force have become 'stabilised' (Clarke, 1977a). This process has advanced much further in South Africa, where the rural labour force has begun to shrink significantly. In conditions of forced resettlement, many black workers have been packed off from the farms where they lived under feudal conditions to the greater freedom (from constraint), if not prosperity, of semi-urban settlements in the Bantustans. According to Merle Lipton, it is sometimes the state that holds up expulsions farmers desire until space somewhere in an over-crowded Bantustan is located for them (Lipton, 1986). Some then return to farms on a seasonal basis while long-distance migrant labour has become less important. On the farms the less-skilled work is done by women while there is a significant growing pool of skilled and better-paid male labour that can run tractors and other expensive machinery. The social conditions of southern Africa continue to ensure a large pool of agricultural wage labour but the development of agrarian capitalism has meant that nonetheless the pool has become smaller and more sharply differentiated. Kerstin Leitner has emphasised for Kenya that agrarian labour is still tending *not* to become more stabilised in the big estates; she believes that seasonality prevents this from being the most efficient or profitable way for rural capitalists to operate (Leitner, 1976).

The penetration of capitalism into African agriculture brought about the creation of massive migrant labour systems, often bigger even than those that we associate with foreign-owned mining ventures. Where migration essentially fed African owned farming systems, however, it has often become assimilated into older, culturally sanctioned forms of labour clientage and patronage and retains extensive possibilities for the migrant to feel something other than entirely proletarianised. Thus, the inner savanna of French West Africa, especially the present-day republics of Mali and Guinea, provided workers for the groundnut export production of Senegal, continuing a pattern from the pre-conquest days of slave production. In the cocoa fields of the colonial Gold Coast, a large force of landless labourers came from the northern part of the colony or beyond, in Upper Volta, Niger or Nigeria, but they generally aspired either to acquire cocoa land of their own or to use their savings to expand their chances at home. They were generally treated as sharecroppers, with the right to a share of the cocoa that they harvested. It is hard to ascertain to what extent a permanent rural proletariat exists but large farms dependent on hired and share cropped labour, produce an important share of the cocoa crop.

One of the largest such systems existed in the Sudan, where the 'tenant farmers' of the Gezira, who produced the largest export crop of African cotton outside of Egypt, depended on the labour of many seasonal workers, as did the food farms of the rainfed agricultural belt further south. A huge well-articulated system came about by the time of independence in 1956 which to some measure harmonised subsistence food and pastoral production with the market-orientated sectors of the rural Sudanese economy (O'Brien, 1983). This system, like others typical of colonial formation, is no longer well-articulated as the need for cash advances has made cultivators and pastoralists become too profoundly dependent on needs that they cannot meet. It is this that leads to a rural proletarianisation rather than any inherent need by capital for cheap wage workers on the land. The issuing forth of a surplus labour-force actually reflects not the needs of capital but a growing social crisis on the land, even though it may register as a more 'productive' agriculture measured in terms of land usage.

It may also be argued that the most effective capitalist development in tropical Africa has occurred in conjunction with the stabilisation over a long period of a market-orientated 'middle' peasantry. One classic line of Marxist theory has always seen the 'middle' peasantry as tending to dissolve under the pressure of market forces into a wealthy minority that would become rural capitalists or kulaks and an impoverished majority of wage labourers, perhaps drifting into town if it can. This has been much less the case in Africa than one might imagine. The rural population tend to cling to some land and are not easily entirely deracinated. The political conditions of post-independence Africa have been discouraging for investment in farming and land. The most successful cultivators have branched into money-lending, rack-renting in the city and pouring savings into education for children who can then aspire to posts in the civil service (and, thus, in effect the ruling class); they do not seek to become improving farmers. The case has been made that the survival of a middle peasantry, able to harvest a surplus on the market and to do without any significant dependence on wage labour, provides food and industrial commodities at a bargain price and serves as an underpinning for social stability. It may be a desirable partner for industrial capitalism and has the resources under the right conditions to thrive indefinitely. Kenya has been given attention particularly as the site of such a middle peasantry and this in turn helps to explain the relative political stability of the conservative Kenyan state since independence. Other interpretations by Kenyan scholars have rather argued for the growing relative dependence on wage labour and for the generalised use of the peasantry as a cheap workforce (ROAPE, 1981, 20). Nonetheless, all agree on the importance of the survival of this class for the social structure as a whole.

The prospects for capitalist social and economic forms to develop within the framework of contemporary agrarian African conditions are clearly variable and a variety of trends can be discerned. We would understand them better if we could make more sense of agriculture as a labour process itself. One important aspect of this labour process which equally affects such activities as fishing or mining but not secondary industry is environmental. The question of the seasonality of work needs as a result of the changing rainfall and temperature, the quality of soils and how best to work them, the lay of the land, obviously plays a major role in understanding how best to assess economic development in agriculture. During the colonial period, agricultural 'experts' tended to be far too ready to prescribe apparently efficient and productive techniques more or less forcibly to African peasants while assuming that the traditional work methods were simply backward, reflecting ignorance and fear.

In reality, the peasants often had a more sophisticated knowledge of how to deal best with the particular conditions, often of considerable infertility, prevailing in African conditions. Moreover, the peasant was logically more concerned to find the minimum labour-time expenditure suitable for his household needs than to create the most productive form of agriculture from the point of view of the natural environment or, more to the point, the market. The coming of colonialism to highland zones in West and East Africa characteristically meant the decline of labour-intensive terrace agriculture on hillsides, which looked tidy, garden-like and very productive to European experts, for labour-extensive cultivation of staples on the plains that enabled households to disperse and allowed for the insertion of various more efficient means, including migrant labour, of procuring cash.

Liberal economic theory has tended to assume that peasants in Africa were simply awaiting the arrival of colonial peace and the railway or road to start producing for the market. This is the theory of 'vent-for-surplus' which assumes that peasant production just requires a convenient vent to yield a suitably marketable surplus. In the sophisticated construct of W. Arthur Lewis, this implied that economists could conceive of early twentieth-century tropical Africa as possessing unlimited supplies of labour, with more productive techniques only really relevant once that supply became more differentiated and scarcer (Lewis, 1954). In practice, though, authors such as John Tosh have explored in some depth the question of colonial cash crop production expansion in terms of shifts in traditional labour usage (Tosh, 1978). Through balancing new crops and expansion of old ones with the seasonal rhythms, organising communal work parties, intercropping possibilities and the injection of cash, adjustments that could ultimately be quite momentous to rural communities were made. Tosh also looks at the environment to explain why the cash crop phenomenon varied so much between different sections of the continent (Tosh, 1980).

Although this assessment gets us quite a long way, it is possible to see it as still overly technicist in character. Thus Jane Guyer has expressed concern that we are still masking questions of social power in understanding internal peasant relationships. 'One could . . . legitimately claim that farm organization is a function of the organization of work, one's own and others' (Guyer, 1982). Guyer suggests that the physical environment as well as the set of tools used are still insufficient to explain how power in rural society works. In short, the key to understanding rural labour is to discard for most purposes the model of the peasant family and peasant society for a more penetrating analysis that is based on internal as well as external power relations, a great potential range of adaptations and an actual look at how work in agriculture is structured as *work*.

While it might seem at first sight that urbanisation and direct subjection to market production would have brought about a class of workers that could be relatively easily understood and subsumed under the categories of capitalist industrial society familiar to Westerners, there are problems equivalent to those to be found in comprehending labour on the land in the African city. With the exception of South Africa, which needs special treatment precisely for this reason, only a small section of African workers actually are wage workers operating in the sphere of mass commodity production. Nor is this section growing very significantly. A conservative team estimate of the working population of the Nigerian metropolis of Lagos in the 1970s suggested that only a minority were to be found registered as wage workers (Fapohunda and Lubell, 1978). In a city such as Lagos, which predates colonial rule and represents to some extent a continuation of pre-industrial economic forms, this is perhaps less surprising than the burgeoning in formerly well-ordered colonial cities such as Nairobi and Lusaka of what social scientists negatively and ineptly term the 'informal sector'.

The state in colonial times and often thereafter has taken an ambiguous stance at best towards the 'informal' sector of the economy and those who work within it. Classic development strategies focussed on industrialisation and its consequences in an urban context or the development of a prosperous peasantry in a rural one. The world of shanty towns, of corner stalls and makeshift sweatshops, of women selling little packets of flavouring for stew, individual cigarettes and bars of soaps did not belong to the structures that it proposed and planned. It was supposed to be a mark of backwardness and a temporary phenomenon only. In reality, though, it is precisely the 'informal sector' that has flourished most in post-colonial Africa and any serious assessment of the African worker has to give to it a serious share of attention.

However this situation has changed from the point of view of international scholarship and the international aid nexus very considerably. Whereas 'informal activity' was once seen as parasitical, marginal and semi-legal, it began to be suggested that the dense network of activities covered in this category actually succeeded in mopping up unemployment, in providing goods and services extremely cheaply for a poorly-paid population (whose poor pay provided one in a very small array of internationally competitive features that sometimes attracts trade and investment to 'developing' countries) and who in effect soaked up political and social discontent in a way so as to prevent urban proletarian revolution. From those who experienced exploitation only in an indirect and rather indigenised form, there was little reason to expect an anti-capitalist explosion. Within the 'informal' sector there was the possibility of entrepreneurial success for an individual with no qualifications or formal education. At its most beneficial, the 'informal sector' constituted Africa pulling itself up by its own bootstraps. Indeed foreign aid agencies have become interested precisely in ways to assist and structure its development, albeit largely in vain.

The picture offered by the 'informal sector' is in fact a largely contradictory one. A perceptive scholar notes that

detailed observations of 'informal sector' activities always reveal great vitality, considerable technological developments and every sign of responsive and adaptable growth, while the larger picture remains one of a seemingly endless perpetuation of the sector and its problems of poverty and low productivity. (Bienefeld, 1975, 73)

From the perspective of labour, the informal sector hides an enormous amount of exploitation of an extreme kind.

There is a need to take apart the whole concept of 'informal sector' based as it is on a rather artificial notion of how the African economies actually work and try to reconceptualise it. In so doing, two particular sectors appear within it. One is the immense sphere of commerce and services particularly geared towards the needs of poor urban dwellers. The countryside no longer can serve as the seat of cheap reproduction of the wage labour force as a whole. Goods pass through many hands and can be sold in locations and quantities suitable to the poor but unprofitable to large-scale operations given their fixed costs. Secondly, the 'informal sector' embraces the myriad of productive activities that take place outside the factories. In many parts of West Africa particularly, the provision of shelter, food, clothing as well as the most basic amenities and such articles as furniture come primarily from workshop production.

The relation of small-scale artisanal production to factory production is by no means entirely clear. Is the factory marginal in the African context or is the artisan marginal in the global one? Those who emphasise the latter aspect focus on the dependence of the artisan for supplies, stock and the basic form that prices take on the 'formal' sector, typically dominated by multi-national corporations either on their own or in co-operation with the state. Those who focus on the former concentrate on the extent to which only small-scale producers actually succeed in providing for the crucial requirements of the working population at large for social and physical reproduction. Some have argued for the low wages of 'informal' activity serving capital by pulling workers' wages down in general. Interestingly, while Philippe Hugon, surveying the 'informal sector' in the Malagasy capital of Tananarive, attributes its development to the stagnation of the post-colonial economy, Sara Berry, looking at the motor mechanics of the Nigerian city of Ife, considers that the opposite is the case. It is precisely the prosperity of Nigeria in the oil boom years which enabled the production, repair and commercial nexus of the 'informal sector' to burgeon. In a city of 100,000 + inhabitants with virtually no mass production firms, Ife boasts perhaps 1,000 motor mechanics (Hugon and Berry in Coquery–Vidrovitch, 1983).

Still another approach would involve emphasising the incomplete nature of the transition to capitalism in Africa. Particularly in West Africa, petty production often contains many survivals of social forms that regulated the organisation of economic life in pre-conquest soceieties; 'guilds' in the region of modern Nigeria as well as the so-called castes of the western half of the sub-continent. Neither system was precisely orientated to the organisation of labour but they reflected its incorporation into relations of kinship, patronage and links to merchant capital. Formal guild and caste structure took on articulation in part through their relation with the state and this aspect was lost with the colonial conquest yet the new economic impulses of colonial society gave to it the possibility of continuity. Much of the tradition of craftsmanship among blacksmiths in Kano, Nigeria has actually survived into the modern era (Jaggar, 1973). Berry's motor mechanics are incorporated into a network of apprenticeships concerned to regulate entry into full-scale workshop ownership. Apprenticeship masks the exploitation of the labour of youth in a culturally fulfilling way. This network transcends religious and ethnic differences in Ife but has a considerable relation to the way guilds once worked in Yoruba country. In Senegal, castes arose perhaps as a means of organising labour in the interests of servicing the old ruling classes but they have adapted themselves and survived the demise of those classes, colonialism and its aftermath and the impact of large-scale urbanisation. Old crafts have themselves surprisingly survived and reconstituted themselves (Nguyen Van Chi-Bonnardel and Diouf, both in Coquery–Vidrovitch, 1983).

The relationship of production to commerce is an intimate one, as it was in pre-conquest Africa. Merchant capital was in a strong position to control specialised forms of production and acquire the lion's share of profits in them. It may be true that this remains the case.

One area of labour where pre-capitalist forms meet with other features of the 'informal sector' lies in domestic service. There is very little written on domestic workers in Africa apart from southern Africa but it is an important part of the sphere of domestic reproduction and often involves the exploitation of an outer circle of relations through use of kinship obligation systems and of children. In southern Africa, there is a significant study of Southern Rhodesia, where the majority of 'servants' have been male. Their working conditions have been covered by the Masters and Servants Ordinance, which has striking pre-industrial, almost feudal, features such as the legal obligation that servants had to accompany masters if requested anywhere within the country, and the generally applicable penal sanctions that could be applied against breach of contract (Clarke, 1974b). The impermeability of exploitation comes forth strongly in Jacklyn Cock's remarkable book, *Maids and Madams*, which illustrates the intertwining of personal and work relations, the isolation of the servant and her inability to express her grievances to her employer (Cock, 1980).

Domestic workers rarely organise effectively against exploitation or poor wages and this seems virtually inherent in their conditions of labour: isolated, surrounded by others pounding at the door looking for work. This is in effect a general characteristic of the 'informal sector'; it is hard to organise. It is equally difficult to create a revolutionary theory around the activities of the urban poor in general.

Taking a leaf from Frantz Fanon's electric classic, *The Wretched of the Earth*, many political theorists have speculated on the potential of the urban crowd as a political force. This represents in large part a specific rejection of the classic view of the unionised mass production worker as the undoer of bourgeois society. According to Fanon,

> It is within this mass of humanity, this people of the shanty towns, at the core of the lumpenproletariat, that the rebellion will find its urban spearhead. For the lumpenproletariat, that horde of starving men, uprooted from their tribe and from their clan, constitutes one of the most spontaneous and the most radically revolutionary forces of a colonized people. (Fanon, 1963, 129)

Yet Fanon himself went on to express a clear awareness of the extent to which the lumpenproletariat on its own could be used by the forces of reaction. And what happens to the politics of the lumpenproletariat after the coming of independence? The post-colonial state has found that irregular men and women, irregular shelter, irregular occupations that escape its gaze, are not so useful. In consequence, it has been characteristic of many independent African states that hawkers and street-sellers are hounded, that market women are blamed for the problems of the nation and that shanty-dwellers, exactly as in South Africa, are forcibly removed and sent back to the countryside (Miti, 1985; Robertson, 1984).

In practice, those who work in the 'informal sector' are well aware of the gulf between rich and poor and they are capable of reacting politically against a regime that seems to pass the bounds of what is acceptable. However, the very wealth of patrimonial networks and the prevalence of pre-capitalist ideology makes the 'informal sector' an unlikely source of sustained or coherent resistance to an unjust order. The importance of understanding what goes on within it must lie not from a faith in it as a revolutionary alternative to the classic proletariat but as a witness to its central role in the realities of contemporary African capitalism. Shed of the colonial carapace, it is the multifarious mercantile networks and the web of personal services and efflorescence of petty production systems that make capitalist accumulation operate in Africa to a major extent. There is little reason to see these activities as being in any imminent danger of being vanquished or effectively subsumed either by mass-production capitalism or by the state. Instead, to understand the character of labour within its boundaries, we need to be more aware of its own capacity for a dynamic of growth and to learn more about how such a dynamic actually operates (de Miras, 1984).

The work that African women do has been too easily excluded from studies of labour in Africa. African women are represented relatively poorly among factory workers, white-collar and skilled employees, as skills are conventionally defined, although their numbers are tending to increase. They are crucial to much of the so-called informal sector, however, and they perform most of the agricultural labour in many sections of Africa. Consequently, the situation of women is central to understanding labour in agriculture and in petty craft production and commerce. In addition, however, it is important to stress that in fundamental respects, the relation of women to the family and to men has often been very different in Africa than in the European model often applied with little alteration or reconceptualisation.

One very influential model that is frequently invoked to explain women's labour in the broader context of the household is that associated most definitively with the French anthropologist Claude Meillassoux, touched on in chapter 1. Meillassoux posited an African household in which the labour of slaves, clients, youths and women (who could, of course, be identical with any of the first three categories) is controlled by and the product redistributed by, male elders. Given the importance of women as farmers, their exploitation becomes central to the picture. Marriage becomes a question of exchanges over labour between male-dominated kinship groups. While women's work includes to an important extent household duties, childrearing and activity associated with the reproductive faculties of the household, women's work is directly and equally crucial to the actual production activities as well. Exploitation is closely to be associated, of course, with the operations of class society and some writers have insisted on seeing women therefore as an exploited class, or semi-class.

With this class model there are some real problems but its strength is certainly in pinpointing the realities about the heavy workload that African women bear, notably in the rural context. Over a wide range of African societies, studies have found that women's labour involves a far greater number of hours over the day or the year than that of men and, at the same time, women retain a disproportionately small proportion of the product of their labour. The finding from Ghana by one writer that 'it is the women who control the commanding heights of the town's economy' (Hagan in Oppong, 1983) is most unusual. Mona Etienne's conclusion that among the Baule of the Ivory Coast, 'men have their cash crops, often lucrative, and women's share in the profits is disproportionate to the considerable labour they contribute', (Etienne in Oppong, 1983, 304) is more typical. In a case study from the vicinity of the Cameroonian capital of Yaoundé, Jane Guyer learnt that the traditional domination of women in agriculture altered very substantially when cocoa was introduced successfully as a cash crop. Men then entered into cocoa production and became far more successful than the women in gaining access to cash while women were confined largely to the production of food crops. As the Yaoundé market grew, however, food crops began to be a business as well and women were beginning to fare much better as a result. However, male farmers and merchants were consequently acquiring an un-traditional interest in the farming of staples. It is also difficult to disagree with Jeanne Henn that there is nothing in the actual exertion of labour or in the imperatives of biology that can really justify or explain why women are not able to do better in agrarian Africa (Henn, 1982).

On the other hand, there are a number of important objections to be made to the Meillassoux model. One is that it fails to allow for forms of inequality apart from gender. There is little reason to think that all women have equal difficulties and that there aren't women who have acquired the right or power for far more control over their own lives, leisure and even power over others than the model suggests. Claire Robertson has suggested that if West African slaves in pre-colonial times were largely women (their market value was very typically higher than for men), they were also largely supervised within the household by other women. Household labour was largely organised by them. This is why it is difficult simply to see women as a class.

In addition, it is a tricky business to generalise for sub-Saharan Africa as a whole on the question of women and labour exploitation. In practice, the rights of women to the product of their labour and the extent to which they could take advantage of a range of opportunities vary enormously. In some respects, the economic possibilities open to women were greater than according to the norms of European or Asian society; this is the other side of the question of the heavy workload. In much of Africa, women have long played a key part in the world of commerce, especially short-distance commerce. Many parts of what is today Nigeria retain traditions of women market officials, including the Muslim north where women were in time to become officially secluded. Perhaps the question of seclusion, which is so easily associated with extreme forms of control and oppression, itself needs to be dwelt on further. Writers such as Renée Pittin have shown that a large proportion of Muslim Hausa-speaking women in the northern parts of

Nigeria actually choose to live considerable portions of their lives as free women, between marriage and without husbands. They are considered in some measure as prostitutes (*karuwai*) (Pittin in Oppong, 1983). However, they in fact engage in other activities to support themselves and are best understood simply as women who live independently of men and support themselves. Among married secluded women in urban Hausa communities, Enid Schildkrout has written about the prevalence of extensive trading networks that proceed independent of male-dominated commerce. The secret of how secluded women can engage in commerce, notably in prepared food, lies in their ability to exploit the labour of children who can engage in the selling (Schildkrout in Bay, 1983).

Thus even in a part of Africa where it is not thought of as respectable or proper for a woman to engage in agriculture, she works as a matter of course and does not think of serving as an adjunct member of the household relegated primarily to the sphere of reproduction. Nor is her work, as might have been often the case in European craft production, part of her husband's activities. From this one can come to two important points which are necessary for qualifying the Meillassoux model. One, true as well for other parts of the continent, is that 'all West African women work, and that most work longer hours and engage in more physical labour than men. Work in the sense of playing an economically productive role, is central to the self-image of women . . . Women do not expect to be, or want to be, dependent' (Ware in Oppong, 1983, 17).

Katherine Abu, writing about Asante in Ghana, considers that 'the most striking feature of the marriage relationship in Ashanti is the separateness of spouses' resources and activities and the overtness of the bargaining element in the relationship' (Abu in Oppong, 1983, 156). The men and women she interviewed in her research found that the idea of pooling their business activities was bizarre and undesirable. The other point, is that in Ghana and many other parts of Africa, marriage does not dominate women's lives in the sense that they might expect to spend most of it in a joint household with a male head. In practice, they only spend parts of their lives in this condition. Much of the time, women head their own households. One reason is polygyny. The strength of polygyny, which formally or informally has proved remarkably resilient in Africa despite the onslaught of Western ideology, enforces the idea of the real household productive unit as consisting of a woman and her children, whose relationship to the broader family nexus is complex and subject to bargaining considerations. It has become tempting for feminist writers to see Africa as a continent where 'patriarchy' is writ large and where women's chances for work and opportunities of independence are the result of collective struggle against such a patriarchial authority but if this is the case, it must be acknowledged that such struggles are deeply imbedded in ancient forms of kin and work relations and that they have taken different forms and had different outcomes in different areas. Broadly speaking, moreover, the male-centred European family model is not a very apt indicator of how these structures evolved in Africa.

A new and very significant area of inquiry is opened up if one considers the situation of women in urban areas. In the urban context, it remains true that women function apart from being adjuncts to a primary family unit and that they count on doing productive work, often outside the home, to make a living which is not pooled into a broader family fund. Yet the possibilities for wage employment amongst African townswomen have generally been poor. Women tend to form only 5 to 10% of factory employees on average. Although it is important not entirely to discount the small number of women who have acquired specialised educations and made good careers on that basis, often careers already defined in the West as being partially or entirely the province of women (nurses, primary school teachers, secretaries), it is not here that opportunity usually lies.

Instead, women's lives in urban Africa have been closely related to the efflorescence of the informal sector and the provision of services allowing for the short-term urban daily reproduction of labour-power even where the more long-term process was still largely confined to the countryside (Chauncey, 1981). With the intensification of urban life in the past twenty to thirty years, the role of social reproduction in the city has become progressively more crucial. This is a part of the assessment that Luise White has made in her important study of prostitution in Nairobi during the colonial period. Whereas prostitutes of course constituted a group of women who provided for the sexual needs of men in a setting where the wives remained back on the farm, they also were involved in the provision of other basic services which capital either did not allow for or only in a clumsy, uncompetitive and expensive way (White in Cooper, 1984).

White is only one of a number of writers who have emphasised that women came to African cities not merely as housewives but on their own searching for an escape from the drudgery and exploitation of rural life and for release from oppressive family situations. Within the rural household, for which our models are far too functional, there have been inherent conflicts and tensions that the impact of the cash economy has both heightened and allowed for the possibility of escape. Urbanisation and the possibilities offered by the sale of services and commercial goods as much or more than wage labour create the possibility, according to some writers, of liberation from the oppressive characteristic forms of African patriarchy. As such women experience the classic travails and new horizons of proletarianisation. According to Deborah Bryceson, writing on Tanzania,

Women workers could be generally characterized as independent women who perhaps rely on boyfriends to pay their rent and on members of the extended family to look after their children, but who ultimately depend on the sale of their own labour power to maintain themselves and their children, and thus to some degree they have succeeded in overcoming the sexual subordination they suffered as peasants. (Bryceson, 1980, 26)

A study of a proletarian quarter of Dakar revealed that it was often women who achieved more success than men at finding a niche in the urban economy. Many cases were recorded of female factory workers, petty traders and domestics supporting unemployed husbands, a situation which tended to weaken marriages and push even more intensely on women the need to produce goods and services for cash (Kane, 1977).

Much of the current literature available on the social history of the West during and following the Industrial Revolution has emphasised the evolution of a new kind of urban working-class family based economically on the male breadwinner assisted by his housekeeper–wife. In Africa, by contrast, most available material suggests that the impact of urbanisation and the prevalence of the cash economy there has tended to destabilise marriages and challenge the dependent links binding women to husbands and, perhaps more critically, to wider kinship groups. In this case, the ideas of Marx on the subject, that the Industrial Revolution would herald the death of the earlier type of family, seems more borne out in Africa than in Europe.

As Kane suggests, conflict between men and women seems to intensify in the urban setting. One of the remarkable pieces available on the subject lies in the work of Claudine Vidal on the Ivorian capital of Abidjan and women's lives there. In Abidjan, women struggle to achieve a maximum of cash income and independence and this largely involves realising ambitions in the 'informal sector'. The most successful women are in fact entrepreneurs and women aspire to possess their own businesses. However, paradoxically this goal of independence is best achieved through relationships with men. The colonial character of Abidjan comes out when one considers that the highest form of this pursuit lies in winning the favours of a white man, who is likely to be less adept at manipulating the woman. The African man attempts to impose his own dominance, economically and socially, on women through the re-impositions of the values of the village coupled with those associated with European culture (Vidal, 1977).

This should not suggest that women's lives in town are purely to be seen in terms of progress and self-improvement. Most women eke out a very poor living for which they work hard and their obvious dominance in many areas, most notably West Africa in small-scale commerce, does not make for wealth for the great majority. In her study of Accra women, Claire Robertson emphasises the injustice involved in convenient male hostility to exploitation at the hands of putatively all-powerful market women. 'Nowhere more', she writes, 'than in that attack on Makola market which was safe because the traders have become politically powerless, is the attempt of reconstituted male authority to restore authority over uppity lower-class women more evident' (Robertson, 1984, 285).

Robertson also pays considerable attention to the theme of female solidarity and co-operation, of particular importance because of the tendency in southern Ghanaian society for women to live away from men most of their lives. Such solidarity is particularly noticeable and of economic significance in older cities such as Accra where craft and commercial structures in some form represent a continuity that goes back for generations and reciprocal relationships not easily explicable in capitalist terms have a considerable depth, much like the craft, caste and guild links that have equally survived in West African cities. She also reports that such solidarity is gradually being replaced by a more alienated and isolated existence with the intensification of market relations.

Outside of commerce, a major sphere of women's work in urban Africa has lain in domestic service. Domestic labour has traditionally had a close relationship to non-cash ties deeply rooted in African society such as kinship hierarchies and slavery; exploitation has been linked to patronage and some form of mutual, if unequal reciprocity. This has not ceased to be the case but a more systematic domestic labour has been more and more prevalent since the coming of settlerdom in particular and colonialism in general and it has far from disappeared as a result of independence. The conditions of domestic work are not well-known or often studied despite its enormous scale. Most of the work on the subject that has been done concerns southern Africa where it has systematically been associated with racial subordination as the large majority of servants are blacks working for whites. Here conditions are extremely variable and depend on a big range of personal circumstances although there is a sharper line between wage and non-wage work and less continuity with other forms in which personal services are provided. In general, domestic workers provide their labour for exceptionally little money at exceptionally long hours and with very few vacations or breaks. In general, they must themselves find means of organising the rearing of their own children. This may involve the use of elderly members of the family but increasingly, such individuals themselves establish child care services on a large scale in the African townships. It is difficult for isolated women domestic workers to come together in an organisation or trade union or to find any effective way to fight for better conditions or wages (Cock, 1980 and 1987). There is quite a bit in common between the work domestic servants do and the commercial and productive labour of women in the streets beyond, but in general, the opportunities for access to cash and for community are greater on the outside for all the limitations that do exist.

In general, labour history and labour studies may often be faulted for failing to consider the broader context in which labourers live, how food, shelter and other basic needs get satisfied, what happens outside the paradigmatic factory or office situation. However, in the African context, this is where most labour happens. Nor can one understand the nature of work relegating the family to the shadows behind the working adult male. Classic capitalist work relations exist within a context whereby goods are produced and exchanged and ideas about society and politics formed in rather different ways. Even if we want in the end to come back to basic themes of proletarianisation and the operations of trade unions, we must do so by recognising this wider reality.

❦ 5 ❦

TRADE UNIONS, WORKERS
AND THE STATE

In the generation after World War II, organised trade unions were able to play a strategically effective role in the unravelling of the colonial state in Africa. This was true despite the limited scale of trade-union membership and the very limited extent of industrialisation in the colonial economies. One reason was the economic conjuncture. The rapid growth of African cities and the expansion of world trade once the war was over imposed strains on urban living conditions that made pre-war wages totally inadequate. The ability of workers to rely on a rural subsistence base was also significantly diminished. Of equal relevance was the raw character of social life in the shacks, shantytowns and overcrowded state-built housing. These had not yet come under the effective control of chiefs or landlords with political power or any form of patronage system. The labour movement thrived on the welter of practical grievances and the absence of recourse to less militant activity.

The trade-union movement succeeded typically in organising manual and semi-skilled workers in the docks, on the railways, the post offices, as well as on mines and plantations but it also frequently contained skilled and white-collar sectors: office workers, clerks and teachers as well as supervisory staff. These workers also had economic grievances but they frequently were as much concerned by racist differentials in payment, promotion and treatment that suggested radical objection to the colonial state. This stratum found its future prospects in the developing nationalist movements whose agitation they helped to sustain. The result was a sort of class alliance within the trade unions reflecting at once the militancy of a profoundly unincorporated working class and the increasingly effective obstructionist politicking of those whose co-operation the colonial regime needed to win over if it was to continue with its development plans and post-war ideas of administration.

Trade unions had begun to achieve legal recognition in the decade before the war. In the British Empire, enabling legislation was envisioned by the Labour government that came into power briefly in 1929 but little happened at first. It was a major wave of strikes within the empire, notably in the West Indies, late in the 1930s, that brought the Conservatives towards a policy of legalising, registering and organising trade unions. In 1938 the Colonial Office began to employ its first permanent labour advisor. Most British colonies in Africa then took steps in line with this (Kenya, 1937, Nigeria, 1941, for instances). From 1942, Trade Union Congress employees were seconded to the Colonial Office to help structure the new unions. The pattern in French colonial Africa was more overtly dependent on changes in regime. Union legalisation was authorised by the Popular Front government that won the election of 1936 and withdrawn again under Vichy only to be restored with the liberation of France.

The trade unions were important both because strikes in strategic sectors could cripple the extractive economy and the normal running of administration and because of their potential for organisational discipline and application which was often lacking in other kinds of associations. As a result, there was a marked struggle for political control of the trade unions in the colonies, especially British and French ones, in immediate pre-independence years. One level of this was Cold War competition between rival international trade-union federations. At a less global level, nationalist movements would typically intervene in support of militant strikes at certain junctures and try to bring in the intensity of worker resistance to authority to their own ends. At a yet narrower level, the trade-union leadership was often coveted by ambitious politicians who were impressed with the power base that the movement potentially offered.

Tom Mboya was trained as a sanitary inspector in post-war Kenya. He emerged as the leader of the Kenya Local Government Workers' Union and was the single most important architect of post-Mau Mau African nationalism in the middle and late 1950s. It was Mboya who helped to structure an urban and labour policy that would fit Kenyan workers into an effective political machinery and end the period of potentially revolutionary struggle of the late 1940s. After Kenyan independence, he became Minister of Labour. A parallel, if somewhat less eminent figure, was the Tanzanian Rashidi Kawawa, president of the Tanganyika African Government Servants' Association when the Tanganyika Federation of Labour was created in 1955. While relations between the Federation and the dominant nationalist party, TANU, were very problematic, as we shall see, Kawawa used his union position to become the first TANU member of parliament for Dar es Salaam and, for a time, was a powerful lieutenant in its leadership.

The most important single leader of the trade-union movement at this time in French West Africa was Sékou Touré, who began his working career as a post office clerk after expulsion from a technical college. Touré was the central figure as well in the Parti Démocratique du Guinée which became the ruling party in Guinea after independence in 1958. All of these figures were inextricably linked to trade unionism but none of them consistently espoused working-class politics. Trade unionists in tropical Africa were in a sense brokers between the mass of workers, often profoundly alienated from the corridors of power in the colonies, whether their bosses, the state or the ambitious nationalist movement leadership. In Nigeria, union secretaries often worked several unions as a business and were really petty entrepreneurs; elsewhere, the union leadership was typically drawn from the most educated and articulate sector of the salaried population.

The early appearance of strikes from the earliest days of wage labour makes it clear that this elemental form of labour resistance is in no sense alien to any part of Africa but trade-union organisations were introduced specifically as a means of channelling and controlling workers. Thus the British Trade Union Congress seconded organisers to the African colonies partly to create what were described as responsible, systematic and non-political unions, and partly to combat the incursions of Communist influence. In French colonies, the metropolitan trade unions at first established branches. This did not guarantee that African trade unions would perform as ordered. They were sites of complex kinds of internal struggles. Within the late colonial trade unions, there was neither a pure strand of unhampered militancy nor easily established smooth control by suitable managers. The Mboyas, Kawawas and Tourés balanced relations with their worker constituents and those with business and the state in meeting a range of pressures.

Generally speaking, independence changed this situation by changing the nature of the state and the class interests that it served. In no case was the post-colonial state a workers' state. One might outline the problematic attitude of the state towards the unions as follows:

1. Virtually without exception, African states moved towards as great a control over local social institutions and potential power bases as they could man-

age regardless of their formal ideological stance. The trade union was potentially a nest of rivals to the ruling party and party and state were anxious to ferret out any potentially dangerous leaders.

2. The state thus saw itself, and it must be said that workers were often not unprepared to see it, as the logical and natural patron of the working class. Independence was often followed (some examples would be Ghana, Nigeria, Tanzania and Zimbabwe) by state-decreed wage increases and the expression of hopes that working-class wages could be brought up through legislation to a point where they could support a respectable urban family existence. In this conception of the relation between the state and the working class, the trade union was reduced to functioning as a transmission belt. In return for the state disbursing welfare, the working class could be expected to produce more selflessly in the interests of assisting the state's development effort.

3. African states were committed to an ideology of economic development and to the smooth running of the inherited colonial economy. In general, they took over the late colonial development plans intact. Precisely to the extent that the state was becoming far more deeply involved in economic management through the creation of parastatal companies and through state investment in the economy, wage demands that appeared to threaten profits and the weakening of colonial forms of workplace discipline were increasingly unwelcome. David Cooper has demonstrated that the government of independent Botswana (a country unusual in its tolerance of autonomous civil institutions by African standards) was prepared to intervene forcibly against striking miners. This, he feels, represents the commitment of

the Botswana state to support the profitable investments of foreign corporations. Where the state was itself the object of a strike, the political threat implied in worker action is of course that much more direct (Cooper in Gutkind, Cohen and Copans, 1979). Thus ironically it was often the more left-wing regimes that were apt to be drawn into conflict with independent trade unions.

4. Apart from the virtually natural antagonism towards independent class-based opposition from right-wing regimes eager to enforce a neo-colonial order, there was as well a distaste on the part of much of the African political leadership for a form of consciousness and organisation that seemed to go against both patrimonial channels based on region, ethnicity or religion and that violated the sense of a unified and undifferentiated 'people' on which rested the basis of apparent political unity.

In addition, working-class organisation has suffered from the problems that increasingly beset African economies. While independence at first stimulated the development of a modicum of secondary industry and the number of wage earners increased, the generalised crisis of the 1970s actually led to stagnation or decline. The poor terms of international trade and unfavourable producer prices that led to a corresponding decline in mineral and agricultural exports also affected relevant sectors of wage employment. In general, the weight of the potentially organisable working class in African society has not increased. It is difficult for the trade union to penetrate the burgeoning 'informal sectors', whether in commerce or in production. Economic decline makes organising around effective wage demands difficult even as it discredits the efforts of the state to perform its patrimonial obligations effectively.

There is considerable truth in the claim that the 'despotic' discipline which according to the sociologist Michael Burawoy typified colonial work situations, such as the copper mines of Northern Rhodesia that he studied, did not easily survive independence and the severing of the intimate link between business and a generally accommodating state, committed to furthering capital accumulation where possible. Jeff Crisp has written about the decline of 'scientific management' techniques on the Gold Coast gold mines while Leroy Vail and Landeg White have discussed the collapse of long-established forms of labour control on the sugar plantations of the Zambesi valley in Mozambique (Crisp in Cooper, 1984 and Vail and White, 1980). Once workers understood that patriotic exhortations to keep producing for the good of the nation were going to yield nothing very tangible, these kinds of controls were replaced by much slacker ones. This may in some respects have brought about an easier life for workers but they also have led generally to production decline and with it a decline of the working class in numerical and strategic weight in the economy of much of Africa.

Ghana is an important example to use in demonstrating these tendencies because of the vanguard role Kwame Nkrumah's movement played in the evolution of radical African nationalism, bringing the country to independence in 1957, and because it demonstrates some of the problems surrounding the strength and viability of African trade unions so graphically. There is moreover a relatively well-developed literature on the Ghanaian state and on the organised working class in Ghana which can be summarised readily. Nkrumah created the Convention People's Party in 1949 as a breakaway from the United Gold Coast Convention which had been dominated by the coastal bourgeoisie. Between the UGCC and militant workers there could be little in common. However, in 1950, Nkrumah threw the weight of his formidable new organisation behind the Positive Action strike wave and, in the eyes of the colonial state, union radicalism and nationalist politics merged. This was much less the case in practice over the longer run. The CPP contained many elements including ambitious business interests. Its populism eschewed any clear class position or economic policies. The militant Sekondi–Takoradi docker leader Pobee Biney was brought into the legislative assembly by the CPP from 1951 but he was not comfortable with nationalist politics and applied most of his efforts to critiqueing the CPP for its increasingly cosy relationship with the colonial state and its dilatoriness in bringing about any significant welfare legislation. In the second colony-wide election, Biney was dropped from the ticket and workers began to perceive the CPP as the agency of a new class on the make.

Numerous critics have confirmed the extent to which the CPP was a patronage machine geared up for accumulation but it is also true that, following independence, the party under Nkrumah did increasingly push for radical policies both with regard to the national economy and the international situation of Ghana. At the same time, the CPP regime became progressively more authoritarian and concerned to absorb or to dismantle any alternative sources of power in Ghana. These tendencies figure very importantly in the trade unions. The dominant figure in union politics in the early independence years was John Tettegah, who became Secretary-General of the Ghana Trade Union Congress. According to Jon Kraus, Tettegah led

a pro-CPP wing of the union movement . . . [which] sought to use government and CPP power to several ends: to strengthen the unions through amalgamations and its power in the TUC through centralization; to sharply increase union rights and benefits; and to increase union power in the CPP and government in order to push for more radical and socialist policies. (Kraus, 1979, 267)

Tettegah's strategies fitted the state need for control over civil institutions that might potentially be sources of political opposition; he was most effective at organising the take-over of the leadership of the trade unions, which grew substantially in size and structural coherence and were thought of as an arm the state could use in mobilising people. At the same time, the Ghanaian state under Nkrumah embarked on a major social-welfare programme that aimed through the expenditure by the state of surplus from the earnings of cocoa and minerals to provide for the basic needs of the population. Large-scale expansion of the health and education systems quickly transpired. The trade unions could hopefully be fitted also into a state-led development programme. Thus D.K. Foevie, who had been the best-known militant trade unionist in the gold mine workers' union, was appointed to management after the state purchased most of the privately owned gold mines in Ghana. In a sense it was appointing the reformed thief as the gaoler. Former militant Foevie by 1963 was saying that the union must dedicate itself to 'increased productivity, higher efficiency, more discipline' (Crisp, 1984, 134).

What chance there was of such a strategy working out happily was reduced by the growing strain the Ghanaian economy was experiencing. Producer prices for primary products, notably cocoa, began to fall, the state squeezed producers by offering only low prices through the state marketing boards so as to discourage legitimate sales and enshrine smuggling while the multifold tasks in which an intensely interventionist state was engaging were expanding dramatically in cost. In these circumstances, the actual wages of the employed began to plummet and the welfare facilities the CPP had sponsored ceased to expand and were unable to provide adequate services.

In 1961, the year of the Dawn Broadcast when Nkrumah signalled a dramatic left turn on the part of the CPP regime, the railway workers of Sekondi–Takoradi led a massive strike that secured widespread community support against what seemed to workers an alienating self-contained political apparatus. Thereafter, with repression, worker opposition to the state diminished but it was clear that working-class support for Nkrumah had disappeared. According to Kraus, the influence of Tettegah and those who favoured an administratively powerful trade-union movement as a left force within Ghana diminished as well. Under these circumstances, it was only with the downfall of Nkrumah and the restoration of civilian government after a military interlude that the trade-union movement could recover.

In Anglophone Africa, Tanzania was the country which took up the cudgels for an indigenised form of socialism and radical nationalist politics once Nkrumah fell from power in 1966. Here the pattern with regard to labour was quite similar on the whole. On the mainland, the Tanganyika Federation of Labour, formed in 1955, was at first a remarkably effective and strong body given the weakness of the capitalist economy and the small size of the workforce in this poor colony. Again a tactical alliance emerged with TANU, the principal nationalist movement, which made worker strike action more effective in the first years after TANU and the TFL formed. Problems mounted though from the time that TANU entered the government in 1958, reluctant to acknowledge the legitimacy of autonomous organisations and keen to carry on with the development schemes of the colonial planning departments. By 1960 a TANU minister was intervening in a diamond miners' strike at Mwadui by threatening to support management in mass sackings if the workers persisted, even though the strike had been authorised by the mine-workers' union. Relations between TANU and the TFL then deteriorated and efforts to bring the unions under the control of Tanzanian versions of John Tettegah were not very successful. The TANU government, which took independence at the end of 1961, insisted that the union movement had fallen under the control of an opportunistic leadership that placed wage demands ahead of development goals and was prepared to make opportunist pro-Western international alliances in order to safeguard its own autonomy. In 1964, following its implication (never entirely clear) in a military mutiny whose suppression required President Julius Nyerere to go to the British army for help, the TFL was abolished. As in Nkrumah's Ghana, legal srikes became virtually impossible but the state engaged itself through social policies and minimum wages to work for the institution of a family wage for Tanzanian workers.

Workers were not inspired or interested by the attempts the state made to create trade unions from the top. These structures, reorganised several times, have always suffered from lifelessness and are consequently completely inept at taking up conflictual grievances. When the Tanzanian state, following the Arusha Declaration of 1967, tried to pioneer self-management, workers' efforts to raise questions about conditions or wages were ignored and it was obvious that the management strategy was essentially one of trying to capture worker enthusiasm in order to raise productivity while offering little materially in return.

The conditions in the Tanzanian economy did not allow for a significant improvement in the material rewards for workers as the state would have liked. Starting in 1971, a spontaneous movement, known as the 'Downing of the Tools' swept many factories in the capital, Dar es Salaam. According to Issa Shivji, workers' placards read 'We are ready to work day and night if allowed to take over the factory. For 21 years now from 1952 to 1973, there has been no improvement at the factory. This factory belongs to the workers. It is in Dar not in Persia' (Shivji, 1976, 120). Remarkably, given its extremely backward economic structure, the apparently very advanced issue of workers' control suddenly surfaced on the agenda of political demands in Tanzania in earnest. The state responded with dismissals and support for management, both foreign and local. From the perspective of the Tanzanian state, the answer lay in creating management structures in which worker representation would be significant. The West German model appeared attractive in this context but such structures have not worked effectively within the constraints of the Tanzanian political economy.

The Tanzanian example is by far the best-documented in tropical Africa on the subject and thus useful to investigate but it is not unique. Workers seized factories and experiments in worker-run enterprise have existed in post-colonial Mozambique and Angola and, on a far more fragmentary basis, more recently in Ghana. North of the Sahara, Algeria and, to a lesser extent, Nasser's Egypt were the site of struggles over factory ownership and control and similar experimentation. Such episodes, when they lasted, were not the product of radical regimes confidently planning worker control schemes but the result of abandonment of enterprises by capitalist owners. Worker control was supported as a better alternative than the complete closure of plant facilities. In addition, Africa has been the scene of land take-overs by peasants, relatively well-known in the instance of Zimbabwe where in some areas squatters occupied settler land forcibly, but only known through occasional references in such cases as Uganda in the course of the upheavals it has suffered since the fall of Obote in 1971.

Workers in harness challenge the plans of the state to a degree that has generally proven intolerable. It has been very difficult to make enterprises work well, harmonising the interests of different categories of workers together with the national economy as defined by the class controlling the state. Among recent contenders for flag-bearers of progressive ideology in Africa, Zimbabwe and Mozambique, have also strongly discouraged any independent worker initiatives, taken over existing trade unions and virtually illegalised strikes. Perhaps ironically, it is in rather more conservative states, that allow more leeway to the 'free' interplay of the economy, that the trade-union movement has enjoyed more liberty.

The examples of pre-1966 Ghana and of Tanzania both lend themselves well at first sight to the Butler–Berg thesis which, as we have seen, tried to undercut the view that trade unions were of signal political importance in Africa. Certainly, the Tettegah model of state-patronised trade-union federations functioning as vanguard radical forces within a Left nationalist politics, seems refuted here. However, as has equally been suggested, the trade-union movements of Africa have not all been successfully set aside with ease by nervous states.

In Nigeria, the independent government from 1960 attempted to create a more centralised union movement under bureaucratic control. Despite numerous weaknesses, however, the trade-union movement continued to organise strikes and to challenge state economic policies. The Nigerian state has attempted to act as a patron of labour by setting national wage rates through the example of the public sector following the reports of periodic commissions concerned with wages. These have, however, been followed by strike waves on a national scale, often involving the destruction of property and other dramatic instances of worker resistance, more supported than led by the unions. Thus in 1964, Nigeria experienced a successful General Strike that was the more remarkable in cross-cutting regional and ethnic boundaries just as the country was sliding towards the succession of military coups and the secession of Biafra. The hopes of some Nigerian radicals that the 1964 strike would herald a new kind of class-based politics in the country were not, however, realised. Attempts since the end of the civil war in 1970 to create an effectively top-down, centralised union movement that could discipline the workforce have repeatedly failed. Indeed the idea that the unions could serve as the foundation-stone of a socially radical politics in Nigeria has become more widespread with disillusionment and cynicism over the characteristics of Nigerian politics: clientelism and a vague populist rhetoric.

Richard Sandbrook reached a similar conclusion in studying the practices of Kenyan trade unions, which in theory have been depoliticised by a corporatist-minded state. Union leaders are unable to survive for long in Kenya if they have no real support from their members or if their membership is convinced that they have no real stomach for a fight with the bosses, whether capitalists or state officials. Despite formal state ideology, there is far more turnover in personnel and responsiveness to workers in internal trade-union politics than one might imagine and the unions are far from inert.

It may be argued that it is the continued militancy and low level of social incorporation of African workers that threatens the state and influences the course of public affairs, rather than the structural weight or significance of trade unions, but the former gives to the latter a potency despite their organisational weaknesses and limited size. In Zambia, although the Kaunda government has long since succeeded in institutionalising one-party government, the union movement, and particularly the copper miners' union, retains an autonomy and an adversarial position to the state that is surprisingly vigorous. It is in part the strategic importance of the copper industry, which provides almost all of Zambia's export income as well as the history of the union, well-entrenched before independence, that helps to explain its continuing strength.

Ghana provides an interesting example along parallel lines. Following the overthrow of Nkrumah by police and military forces, civilian rule was finally restored in 1969. The conservative civilian regime of Dr K.A. Busia was no fonder of militant trade unionism than Nkrumah had been but the context of the restoration of civilian rule meant that some liberalisation of union activity was inevitably permitted. However, the main factor in the period was the deteriorating economic situation and the attempt by the state to keep wages low. Studies of the mining sector by Jim Silver and Jeff Crisp indicate that this was a period of unprecedented worker resistance characterised by wildcat strikes of great ferocity and destructive power, involving physical attacks on management in the confines of the small company towns. The union leadership had strongly absorbed state ideology and saw itself at best as mediators between the state, which now owned most mines, and the workers. However, during the wave of strikes, union leaders were themselves attacked and their authority entirely flouted. Militancy flamed within but, to some extent, against the union.

According to Jon Kraus, the characteristic labour figure of the era was Benjamin Bentum, who in 1968 became secretary-general of the Ghana Trade Union Congress. Bentum was an ambitious but genuinely militant union leader. He had been thrown out of the union movement by the CPP regime for exposing corruption and had a disinclination to involve the Ghanaian TUC in politics as it had been understood in Ghana during the classic nationalist era. He wished to concentrate instead on the workers' economic demands and emphasised their organisational independence from party politics and the need to negotiate effectively with the state.

However under Busia, confrontation loomed. More and more intense rank-and-file worker resistance emerged and was met with repression that Bentum was finally prepared to denounce. According to Kraus, Bentum came to see the trade-union movement as 'a workers democratic opposition' (Kraus, 1979, 276). This was never articulated in any coherent political form, though, with any political structure behind it.

As relations deteriorated, in 1971 the Busia government abolished the Ghana TUC and imposed a new series of laws to try to control the unions. Before any clear response emerged, Busia was himself overthrown by a new military regime. There followed a quieter period in labour relations but in the later phases of the Acheampong military era, as the state became more unequivocally authoritarian and while the decay of the Ghanaian economy accelerated, renewed militancy from below again surfaced and again breathed a harsh life into the unions. In 1977–78, an increasingly violent series of strikes affected several mines and threw up a new set of radical spokesmen amongst the workers. Jim Silver has emphasised the failure of mines management to establish order or to deal with the miners' grievances at this point. Only through the unmediated use of state coercion could the miners be subdued. The systematic level of discipline (as measured for instance by the widespread incidence of theft) was very low, indicating the poor control of the work situation at rockface by management and the general collapse of an effective industrial relations machinery.

From following the history of organised workers in countries such as Ghana, particularly interesting because of the range of political regimes experienced over the past thirty years of independence, one can perhaps draw certain conclusions. One is that virtually all African governments have been uncomfortable with strong, radical, independent trade unions. Such organisations violate their own determination to dominate civil society and threaten to function as independent power bases for ambitious politicians and potentially for the emergence of class-based politics. Given the ideology of 'development' and the concomitant alliances with foreign business interests, the state has a strong concern for the maintenance of labour discipline, with the regularity of production and the retention of wage levels that appear to be internationally competitive with a host of other impoverished countries. As such, independent trade unions appear to be a selfish and sectional interest that causes havoc to the fragile post-colonial economy and spearheads the decline in productivity and has gone hand in hand with the decline of the type of work authority that typified the colonial period. Even where the state would like nothing better than to provide a reasonable family wage for stabilised workers, the darkening economic crisis in most African countries has made this virtually impossible and as such has provoked an inevitable confrontation and with it a turn to repressive responses.

Nonetheless, while all this would appear to have spelt complete doom for the trade unions that were occupying a role of some importance on the eve of independence in most African countries, organised workers retained certain strengths that continued to animate them. Where trade-union federations, such as in Ghana (under Nkrumah and again briefly in 1971) or on a far more permanent basis in Tanzania, were smashed and restructured, the result was not very successful from the point of view of the state or business. Particularly in a country like Tanzania where many workers had some guarantee against being dismissed, lifeless, top down unions meant that worker productivity was often low. Worker resistance, instead of disappearing, was dissipated into a variety of informal channels of the classic kind – theft, desertion, poor work habits, etc. – which were very difficult to get around for management. When some touchstone led to an explosion, there was no structure in which workers had any faith to mediate the problems, thus threatening violence and immediate political confrontations. Such explosions have frequently played a role in the overthrow of shaky African regimes.

As a result, union organisation has survived in many independent African countries. Their leaders are often bought out by the state, corrupt, inept or alienated from the mass of workers, but the logic of the trade union's situation means that this often is remedied in time through conflict which throws up new leaders and revives the union as a field of activity. Nowhere has the trade-union movement succeeded in becoming the heart of an effective political movement representing the working class or, for that matter, the generalised poor, but a sensitive analysis of developments in a country such as Ghana also shows that the unions are conduits at times for shocks that can present difficulties for regimes that have removed themselves from such a perspective. Thus unions, if less critical to African politics than some once imagined would be the case, have continued to possess a considerable salience. Kraus argues that such leaders as Bentum (and Richard Jeffries makes a similar case for the old railway and dockers' leadership in Sekondi–Takoradi) are fired by a respect for the 'moral economy of the poor'. Far from being a labour aristocracy, most organised workers in Tropical Africa, particularly those not in clerical jobs, suffer from basic economic grievances and experience the impact and the disappointment of the fading development prospects of the continent. Even where their wages are better than those of others, the communities they live in still benefit materially from their relative good fortune.

Nonetheless unions thus far have notably not captured a more specific class consciousness than the generalised opposition of the poor vs. the privileged (once perhaps, above all, the whites; now, the state and its African beneficiaries).

This places a limit, particularly given the slow increase (where one exists at all) in the industrialisation of production, on the formation of any coherent socialist politics in Africa independent of the schema of educated state functionaries. Unions have been more comfortable with a critical and oppositional role than with forming any kind of nexus for a politics differing from the patrimonial populism that rose to the surface in the late colonial era. Nothing visible by the late 1980s suggests that this situation is particularly apt to change.

❧ 6 ❧

LABOUR IN AN INDUSTRIALISED SOCIETY: THE SOUTH AFRICAN CASE

There are a number of reasons that could justify a special chapter on South Africa alone in this volume. One would be the topical interest raised by expectations of revolutionary transformation of the existing social and political system in South Africa, together with an awareness of the political potential of the organised labour movement, in that transformation process. A second lies in the relatively rich literature, particularly historical literature, available on South African labour by comparison with other parts of the continent. However, the governing principle for putting forth this chapter has been that South Africa requires special attention because of the far-reaching nature of South African capitalism and because, qualitatively, industrialisation has gone so far beyond anything comparable in sub-Saharan Africa. South Africa is the only industrialised country of international consequence in this part of the world although even then one needs to qualify exaggerated claims for its economic autonomy; its transformation to an industrialised society is incomplete. The rise of industrial capitalism in South Africa has been coupled with the dominance of a large immigrant community that came to the region and multiplied in tandem with colonial expansion. There is a relation in this history to the development of other countries where far smaller, less effective but still consequential settler communities came along later, notably Kenya, Zimbabwe, Angola and Mozambique, although there is as well a qualitative difference with South Africa.

In considering the development of labour in South Africa, it seems useful to create an historical periodisation marked by definite watersheds. The first period focusses on the development of a colonial economic system before the mineral discoveries of the 1870s and 1880s. Secondly, one needs to consider the implications for the rise of a labour force to work the mines that became central to the economic history of the region once the working of deep-level gold deposits on the Witwatersrand became both technically feasible and economically desirable to capitalists in the early 1890s. The 'mineral revolution' in turn helped to power, and was in fact a necessary although not a sufficient reason for, an industrial revolution which generalised capitalist production widely throughout the national economy and transformed sectors of the economy such as transport and, to an important extent, agriculture while developing manufacturing. This industrial revolution can be made a distinctive third stage from the time that the heightened profits in gold mining brought about economic recovery after 1933, although it took until the 1960s before mass production became fairly generalised in industry and monopolised in its characteristic South African form. Finally, it may be useful to mark out a fourth stage, the crisis period beginning in the early 1970s when the rapid economic growth of South Africa has largely halted and it is increasingly unclear where the direction of capitalist development in South Africa lies. The current crisis has both economic and political aspects that are extremely difficult to disentangle. Here we will concentrate on the implications for workers particularly.

The first stage represents the first two centuries of European penetration from Cape Town including, in the first two-thirds of the nineteenth century, its substantial expansion north and east. From the point of view of labour history, the most central fact of this period was the failure of any of the states in the region (including those under the control of the British Empire) to generate a skilled, disciplined, proletarianised working class either through the free immigration of colonists or the impact of new political, social, or economic relations amongst the indigenous African population. Small numbers of settlers arrived from Europe over generations and prospered securing a considerable economic independence. Within the colonist community, there did emerge a hierarchy of wealth and privilege. A bottom group can be identified from the eighteenth century who did not succeed in gaining access to land or to their own means of production. However, this group remained a minority given the overall ease of obtaining such access, a minority which lacked any clear political aspiration or capacity for social cohesion as a class.

Despite the loss of land and sometimes herds by the indigenous population, it was too difficult for colonists to supervise large populations and too easy to retreat deeper into the African continent for any large-scale proletarianisation of Africans to take place. Only after a very long history of struggle did the colony at the Cape obtain the permanent service of quite small numbers of Khoisan pastoralists as herdsmen and servants. On the Cape eastern frontier, the despoliation of individuals and households made possible the establishment of an occasional rural wage labour force but it was only with the arrival in the 1820s of numerous refugees from the wars of the Mfecane, the Mfengu, that numbers became more substantial. The Mfengu themselves were often able with time to build up herds and re-establish their independence, often taking up new crafts and commercial agriculture as well in relation to colonial merchant capital. Even after the Cattle

Killing of 1857 brought many destitute Africans to colonial farms, following the disastrous prophecy which had urged them to destroy their own means of livelihood, far more favourable conditions for employers existed but still no big permanent wage force. In the interior, the wandering Boers relied on the forceful incorporation of *inboekselingen* – child 'apprentices' – to form the nucleus of a small labour force. Up to the 1870s, it may be said that the relations of capitalism to the indigenous Africans were in good part those of merchants to petty producers operating within a non-capitalist mode of production and that when Africans came to work for wages, they could often do so under relatively favourable conditions from the point of view of wages and bargaining power as in the case of the early diamond diggings.

The only means through which capitalism could create a more docile and controlled labour force at the Cape was through the forcible introduction of immigrants from distant parts of Africa and from Asia with the status of slaves. This slave labour force came to outnumber the free settler population by the end of the eighteenth century and was the backbone of the landed estates that produced wine and grain in the immediate interior of Cape Town. From 1860, the Natal economy profited from the comparable introduction of free but indentured labourers from India whose capacity to work for themselves was nullified during their first years in South Africa. They were used by a large variety of enterprises in Natal, including the coal mines and railways, but above all, their labour was applied to the sugar plantations of the coastal region. Apart from these two limited cases, colonial agriculture did not thrive in this period as a successful producer for the growing international capitalist economy. Wool, the most successful nineteenth century farm export, was characteristically undemanding of a large pool of human labour. The typical

South African white farmer was more of a trader with the African producer, more of a transport-rider and hunter, than he was a cultivator. Unsurprisingly, the first result of the mineral discoveries that suddenly brought large numbers of people together at distant points in the interior of the sub-continent was greatly to increase the importation of food from overseas. Especially beyond the Cape, the needs of capitalism for labour and its products suddenly outstripped by a long way the historic working out of processes that would yield workers.

The series of mineral discoveries that culminated in the deep-level exploitation of the Witwatersrand, very suddenly brought to bear the weight, on this underdeveloped society, of the most important mining industry in the world from the point of view of technical, capital or labour demands. At least until after World War I, the mines management considered themselves to be desperately short of labour and were constantly seeking to increase their labour force. Some of this labour came from overseas. Miners from the British Empire flocked to South Africa. In part they possessed particular skills that were difficult to acquire that related to the growing complexity of the mechanical apparatus that served the industry; but in part they were simply experienced, inured to the risks and horrors of underground work from growing up themselves in mining communities. The immigrant white miners found themselves in a colonial African environment where wages were low and labour coerced and crudely exploited unless it had recourse to land for farming and herding. Even the local white population, increasingly being forced off the land through economic pressures, at first was warded off the mines and skilled trades through effective exclusion because they were viewed as a serious threat to immigrants' wages. However, this exclusivity was far more extreme and crucial when it came to the mass of indigenous black workers. The

immigrant white miners would have liked to eliminate them
entirely or relegate them to a marginal role in urban and
industrial society and the Labour Party, which began to take
shape before World War I, and most clearly represented the
interests of such miners, pressed for an all-white workforce.
In this they resembled equivalent workers' organisations in
California and Australia, who were succeeding in prevent-
ing capitalists from importing large numbers of poor workers from Asia and kept wages, even for unskilled white men,
high.

Capitalists saw things differently. The labour costs involved in running the mines similarly to those in Western
states of the USA or Australia seemed impossible to meet,
given the constraints on the price of gold, the enormous
capital investments that had to be paid back and the specu-
lative stock market flotations that had to be realised. At an
important juncture, following the British victory over the
Boers in 1902, thousands of Chinese labourers, an equivalent group to the Cape slaves and the indentured Indians of
Natal (still coming before Union in 1910) were introduced
to the mines and were crucial in the restoration of profitability after the dislocations of the war. White agitation had
much to do with the cessation of Chinese immigration by
the time of Union in 1910. Capitalists resorted also to hiring
poor indigenous white men. Cheaper unskilled Afrikaners
were brought into supervisory jobs underground from the
time that the immigrant white miners began to organise and
engage in militant strikes (1907).

However, capitalists generally accepted that the largest
numbers of miners (some 100,000 before the Anglo–Boer
War and 200,000 by the time of Union) that were required to
do the hard manual unskilled work would need to be
recruited from amongst the African population. At first,
African workers were not plentiful enough and had too
much bargaining power; they tended to disappear at incon-

venient times, they would not work for the most cut-throat
of employers and the wages they could command were too
high. As a result, the mineowners engaged in private initiatives as well as the manipulation of state policy to improve
their situation. They strongly supported the retention of
certain 'reserves' where commercial resources were limited
but African families could support their subsistence needs,
thus cheapening the price of labour for sustenance. The
state was encouraged to systematise controls over movement of people, including the notorious pass system, which
was in the early days very largely directed at pushing men
out *towards* the capitalist workplace. A compound system
was established and refined to control the activities of the
miner off the job in the vicinity of the mine. The big mining
houses colluded (although with occasional fallings out
amongst themselves) to establish recruiting networks that
linked up a world of petty capitalists in the cities with
merchants and chiefs in the rural areas. Especially in its first
generation of activity the gold-mining industry was dependent on formal recruiting arrangements with the Portuguese
colonial government in Mozambique, where in a region
which had already provided many migrant workers before
conquest became effective, mine work became the main
source of cash over a wide region. Later, a similar
dependence was structured in the British colony of Basutoland (Lesotho), an enclave within South Africa, and to a
lesser extent, parts of Bechuanaland (now Botswana) and
Nyasaland (Malawi). A variety of localised pressures were
in the end effective in drawing out a growing army of black
miner migrants where mining was given cultural prestige
and was the sole male avenue to cash, even for the increased
reproduction of the rural household. One should finally not
underestimate the generalised capitalist pressure imposed
by such methods as state taxation and the impact of the
market on peasant farming where that peasant farming was

no longer able to expand without cash inputs. In 1913, the Land Act made illegal the further purchase of land by Africans in 'white' areas within South Africa. By the 1920s it was possible for the mineowners to attract a very sizeable unrecruited workforce to the gold mines even though real wages were considerably below what they had been before the turn of the century.

All this is not to say that the mineowners wanted a purely black labour force any more than they wanted a white one. They continued to favour a racial division of labour that was moulded onto labour discipline on the mines. Whites were wanted as supervisors as well as for the practice of genuine skills, just as small numbers of blacks continued to be hired as clerks for less money than whites would demand. The bitter battles that were fought between 1907 and the famous Rand Revolt of 1922 between white miners and bosses (punctuated by an impressively large-scale black strike in 1920) were over the relative numbers of white and black and the effective workplace power of the white miners. They ended with a victory for the mining capitalists who secured a racial division of labour based on a diminished number of rather poorly organised white workers and the elaboration of means of control that had become instituted to structure the work of black miners. Whites continued to monopolise the right to blasting certificates which held the key to the most central operation undergound.

Even today, gold mining is still the core of South African capitalism and historically its revolutionary impact on the entire region is undeniable. However there is a tendency towards collapsing the economic history of South Africa and the situation of labour entirely into the story of the gold mines. The enormous wealth of the mines, and the huge labour force required, engendered a broad range of alternative activities that may have supported the gold mines but had their own differing dynamics. Mining brought about the stimulation of labour connected with labour supply itself and the basic needs of miners, it brought about a revolution in transport and it laid the basis for a rapid process of urbanisation with the multifold activities that the twentieth-century urban economy requires. Mining also created the possibility for capitalist agriculture in many parts of South Africa, because it engendered the creation of an expanded home market.

As an example, one could use the province of Natal, through which an important railroad linked the Rand to the harbour at which the city of Durban rapidly grew. Railway revenues quickly became the mainstay of the Natal budget and in turn financed the construction of branch lines to serve farmers. Sugar and other agricultural products found a substantial commercial (eventually protected) market on the Rand. Durban developed the facilities of a major port and was able to support a manufacturing industry. The coal mines of the provincial interior were profitable on the basis of use by the railway. The prosperity of an erstwhile struggling colony depended on the rise of the Witwatersrand.

From the point of view of labour, it is essential to stress the great variety of work situations that were now called upon to exist. In secondary industry, skilled trades flourished in such areas as printing but particularly in the metal industry which directly served the mines. Here was the province of the unionised white immigrant and his descendants whose skill monopoly tended to protect his interests without the use of a direct colour bar and who favoured trade unions without one. In the coastal provinces, but especially the Cape, there were in fact many skilled workers who were not white and unions were not entirely segregated. At the other extreme, brickmaking, to which at first proletarianised white farmers were drawn, quickly became only one enterprise that employed black workers under conditions not too different from those in the gold mines and no better paying.

When a garment industry based on imported cloth first developed after World War I on the Rand, it came to hire largely unmarried white girls from Afrikaner families whose wages were intermediate between those of black unskilled workers and skilled white men. The Boer War had begun a process that took on steam whereby the majority of white farm families were driven off the land as capitalist agriculture built up. Given the intensifying racist character of South African politics, this became defined as 'poor whiteism' and the state tried, especially after the electoral victory of the National–Labour Pact in 1924 to cater for the poor whites in ways that were consonant with capitalist development in South Africa. Business generally eschewed unskilled white labour despite state pressures so the police force, the post office, the forestry department, public works and the railways became the province, and to some extent are to this day, of poorly educated and unskilled white workers. They were paid far less than the skilled white workmen to whose relatively affluent living standard they aspired.

The African population that came to live in the cities of South Africa were, for a long time, largely concentrated in menial work rather than in secondary industry proper. White families employed large numbers of African males and, after World War I in one city after the other, African females, as domestic servants. Some Africans acquired urban skills early though and others succeeded in servicing the needs of the African population. They were prominent in the 'informal sector' of petty production and service trades from an early date. In general, urban jobs offered superior pay and were favoured over mines jobs. While most miners migrated from beyond the frontiers, Africans who came off the farms of South Africa preferred town work.

It is clear that through the first quarter of the twentieth century, the capacity of the 'Reserves' for market production tended to decline drastically but less clear whether self-sufficiency was not still possible for most households. A mixture of state legislation and economic intervention together with the growing possibilities of capitalist accumulation in agriculture were increasingly allowing for the domination of capitalist social relations on the land possessed by white farmers. The Land Act of 1913 contained a provision directly aimed at eliminating shareholding arrangements and, in some regions, it heralded the deteriorating bargaining power of black squatters and their reduction to the status of tenants. Tenants were obliged to perform substantial amounts of labour together with their families in order to remain on the land at all. However, the transition to capitalist relations on these farms and the reduction of squatters to wage labourers was a very slow, contradictory process. At the same time, where capital investment brought about profitable big-scale farming in spheres such as citrus estates, overt racial legislation suppressing such pre-capitalist forms of labour relations as squatting was less necessary. The growing introduction of machinery from the 1940s decisively finished off the squatters in the central Maize Belt but they survived far longer in other areas such as inland Natal.

Finally, two additional points must be made about South African agriculture. One is that much larger numbers of poorly paid farm workers were retained on the land than might be expected from comparative examples of an increasingly efficient commercialised and concentrated agriculture elsewhere in the world. The other is that all but the most successful of the capitalist farmers relied on paying their workers less than they could earn in the cities or the mines and thus favoured fairly harsh methods of control over population movements as well as access to land. It might also be added that some sectors of agriculture, for instance the Natal sugar fields, relied on migrant recruits much as did the mines, not on a resident peasantry.

The general situation of labour, and of the worker, in South Africa through the first quarter of the twentieth century, was thus a very complex one that was profoundly influenced by racism, colonial conquest and gender specificity but could in fact not be reduced to those features. Race did not automatically determine the worker's rung on the ladder. It is not therefore surprising that there were trade unions that attempted at the time to include members of all races and urban neighbourhoods where poor people of all colours lived cheek by jowl. At the same time, ethnicity and race were increasingly used as political organising principles to try to raise barriers that crossed class lines and to differentiate workers more sharply.

Although the mineral revolution engendered very diversified economic activity on an unprecedented scale, relatively little of it was based on mass production. Only after the excellent gold profits of the 1930s, did this situation change. Between 1933 and 1973, rapid growth in the South African economy involved significant investment in an increasingly integrated and massified secondary industry that became fundamental to the livelihood of fast-growing urban populations. Some of this activity, especially the metal industry, serviced the mines directly, other sectors catered to the consumer needs of the working class while yet others arose in response to successful state policies of import substitution through the imposition of tariff barriers and other fiscal devices. The result can be considered an industrial revolution but one which actually continued to depend on mineral exports, especially of gold, for its international trading position. Particularly in the latter phases, a striking aspect of South African industry lay in the dominance of a few large conglomerates, especially the one emerging around the mining house of Anglo–American. The concentration of capital in South Africa had much to do with the immense funds at the command of the mining houses given the more modest overall size of the economy coupled with the policies of the state which directed investment vigorously into local industry. Foreign investment in secondary industry was critical in certain sectors but most of the push for capitalist industrialisation in South Africa was locally derived.

For labour the main implication lay in the requirement for a large, settled class of semi-skilled operatives and service workers. This class, barring major new immigration into the country, could come only from the African population. Particularly during World War II, large numbers of Africans left the rural areas, especially the white-owned farmland, for the cities and secured jobs as industrial workers and the number grew with each advance in the economy until by 1976, there were 1,362,000 (Nattrass, 1981, 165) industrial workers in South Africa of whom the largest number by far were black males. Whites had been the backbone of most secondary industry until the war but thereafter they were not numerous enough and they commanded wages which were too high. Economic development allowed an increasing number to be brought into office and managerial positions, a phenomenon that also began to affect Indian and 'Coloured' workers significantly as well from the 1960s.

So long as white workers had been the repository of essential skills, they defended their position against capital most effectively along craft lines and this affected their political and social views outside the workplace also, although the growing incorporation of unskilled whites off the farms into sections of the urban workforce added an increasingly racist element. The less skilled depended directly on political protection through racist and ethnically defined senses of community to hold their jobs. However, the age of mass production, dawning by the 1940s and well underway in the boom years of the 1960s, tended to deskill many whites. Whites remained in industry increasingly as supervisors of black labour. A racial divide was used by capital in the interests of the organisation of labour while whites thought in increasingly racist terms in order to justify their own status and improved living standard. Thus on the gold mines it is interesting to note that until the 1930s, white miners were more apt to die in accidents per capita than black miners. Thereafter the position changed. In the following decade, the miners' union was defeated and replaced by one that was directly aligned to the Afrikaner Nationalist movement and to the maintenance of a rigid colour bar in mining. Defence of the colour bar became in time more important even in those unions that remained outside of the Afrikaner Nationalist political orbit.

The position of the old South African Labour Party towards the rise of an urban black proletariat had been exclusionist – get the newcomers back to the rural areas – dominated by a deep fear of their undercutting white wages and destroying the precarious prosperity of the white artisan in a country characterised, as elsewhere in Africa, by cheap labour controlled in authoritarian ways. This view was adopted by Afrikaner nationalists, from the 1940s an increasingly urban political movement, and culminated in the entrenchment of apartheid, a rigid form of the segregation system after the National Party came to power in 1948. Yet the requirements of industry pushed in an opposite direction, towards the stabilisation of a growing black working class permanently established in the cities with all the implications this held for policies in health, in housing and in education. From even before the Act of Union, but especially from the 1920s onwards, there was a tendency to segregate the urban population racially by decree. For Africans, this meant the construction of public housing on an increasingly large scale in 'townships' removed from the city centre and designed for state security. The state and, more equivocally, business were determined to destroy both the interracial centre city slumyards and the uncontrolled squatter settlements on the edges of the main agglomerations.

In the 1940s, the contradictions of segregation became more intense. During this decade, the expansion of job opportunities in the cities coupled with the impact of mechanisation on the farms, led to a large increase in black urbanisation, as elsewhere in Africa and with related pressures on housing and social services. This was an era of mass struggles over transport costs, shack destructions and urban removals. The rise of American-influenced jazz and a press aimed at urban blacks suggest, among other things, that a culturally new working class was forming amongst black South Africans, notably in and around Johannesburg, a mecca that drew its African population from the entire country. The development of commuter townships often did provide improved material conditions for many of the former slum-dwellers but, coupled as it was with intensified political exclusion and the suppression of economic activities that made urban life more palatable and less expensive for the poor, also evoked a great deal of resistance. African women found it difficult to earn a wage except from employment as servants and considerable hardship was engendered by removals. Their beer-brewing activities could no longer go on anywhere near workplaces and brewers were indeed persecuted by the authorities who wished to pay for township development out of taxes on liquor and beer. Washerwomen could no longer service customers in the white suburbs of the cities.

Under the Nationalist government from 1948 the contradictions merely became more intense. Exclusionist rhetoric jarred with unprecedented township construction and the growing provision of basic facilities in primary education and health that made for a class fit for industrial employment. The urban policies of the state required extensive policing as 'influx control' was tightened to intensify the difficulties of blacks moving into town. While the economy boomed, especially after 1960, job creation was not so rapid and there was no longer any desire by employers to lure blacks into towns. The role of the state was to keep them out. Removals, pass raids and a range of police harassment, extensive though they were, were ineffectual in fact in keeping blacks from being urban dwellers. In fact, the difficulties placed on movement to town probably engendered a distancing from the countryside of the town dwellers and deepened their new urban roots. Official policy tended to become more and more extreme in its insistence that the black worker would in the long term only have a future in the reserves, now being agglomerated into ethnic homelands. In the late 1960s, the state established legislation to force industry to move to the edge of the homelands while virtually ceasing to build houses and other facilities for urban blacks. This was the period when it is easiest to speak of a split between the state, determined to forge a geographically 'white' South Africa at all costs and capitalists, who depended on a cheap, available and suitably trained black labour force. Although it was a highly prosperous period, it was also at this time that the seeds began to be sown for a modified industrial policy that could overcome this antagonism and deal with the contradictions of apartheid policies.

From the early 1970s, structural problems became far more prominent in the accumulation pattern that was established in the preceding generation. South African capitalism began to suffer the effects of changes in the world economy that squeezed other semi-industrialised economies such as those of Turkey, Brazil or Mexico as well, while equally experiencing special limitations imposed by the political character of the society. The failure to develop industrial exports coupled with the small and stagnant internal market for most commodities served to limit possibilities for industrial expansion. Import substitution could no longer serve as a practical basis for continued industrial growth and terms of trade began to go against many of South Africa's mineral exports. Even where new investment could occur, it tended to take the form of labour-saving machinery that added to a mounting unemployment problem. The severity of the crisis is perhaps less than that in many equivalent countries, for instance in Latin America, but at the same time the rapid economic growth that seemed mostly unstoppable over a forty-year boom phase is equally a matter of the past.

Migrant labour of men from homelands to cities where they are housed in hostels and subject to severe movement controls was notoriously characteristic of South African economic life although never so prevalent for black industrial workers as it was for miners. However, the urban black population has grown so substantially that there is now an ever-larger pool of unemployed and semi-employed township dwellers; migrant labour is increasingly unnecessary. The rigid influx control policies of the past have ultimately failed. What has occurred is a deflection of rural migrants from the centre cities to squatter settlements on the edge of the metropolitan areas where they live amongst those from the townships unable to get more convenient housing. Much of this urbanisation goes on within the 'homelands', several of which administer sections of metropolitan areas (Bophuthatswana for Pretoria, KwaZulu for Durban, Ciskei for East London). State policy has moved from influx control (abolition of the pass laws in 1985) to 'orderly urbanisation' which aims to reconcile the inevitability of black urbanisation with the retention of the orderly, bourgeois and white character of the city centre as much as possible. Industrial decentralisation continues to be pursued but increasingly the new points of development are not far from the existing urban centres.

A related shift, perhaps of more momentous importance, is the recognition by the state of the permanence of the black working class in South Africa and an acknowledgement that no amount of mechanisation or immigration would uproot it. Before this occurred, the impoverished character of township life and the poor range of services available even for those who could afford more than a subsistence livelihood was a logical consequence of apartheid. For many years, virtually no new state housing for Africans was constructed in South Africa, creating severe shortages. The South African state is now beginning to change gears and to provide facilities for major increases in welfare spending, notably housing. Since the beginning of the 1970s, there has been a dramatic expansion in working-class education with a large proportion of urban blacks now attending secondary school. A related implication is state acceptance of the need for more skills and technical expertise that are appropriate to industrial growth and economic development. Finally, the state has been prepared, since 1979, to recognise and register trade unions that cater for black workers. Original reluctance by Pretoria to allow unions to organise across the colour line and among migrant workers had to be overcome for any industrial relations system to emerge. Thus the state now to some extent distances itself from direct intervention in relations between private employer and worker and has proved itself willing, particularly in secondary industry and on the mines, to tolerate a growing amount of differentiation in the wages and living standards of black workers. These various shifts were heralded in a variety of state commissions whose findings have largely or partly been accepted (Riekert on black urbanisation, 1978; Wiehahn on labour, 1979; de Lange on education, 1981).

According to David Yudelman

The most crucial problems shared by the South African state and large-scale business in the 1980s are how to defuse the revolutionary potential of the work force and how to create jobs on an unprecedented scale. This is strikingly similar to the problems faced in the early part of this century, when the critical political tasks were to incorporate organized labor into the state structure without wrecking the capitalist economy and to create jobs for a dangerously large number of unemployed and radical workers. (Yudelman, 1983, 3)

Yudelman is undoubtedly correct that both the state and big business are interested in the creation of a stable, reasonably paid and politically passive black working class in the cities of South Africa. However, the achievement of such a goal is held back in critical ways. There are barriers involved in tackling the massive poverty of much of that working class penned into townships for blacks only. By contrast with the rest of Africa, the petty production sector of the economy is only marginal in South Africa. There is considerable Establishment-sponsored interest in the 'informal sector' and some faith that a process of state deregulation would enable it to flourish and provide some kind of work for the many who need jobs in the townships and elsewhere. However, small business of all sorts in South Africa meets the competition of a highly capitalised and in some respects very efficient monopoly sector. Why buy from small traders and handicraft makers when discount houses and supermarkets provide services as effectively as in Western cities? It is more likely that small black traders and manufacturers would suffer if all apartheid regulations were to tumble and white businesses could move easily into the black townships.

Apartheid has intensified the process through which marriages have become more fragile and less effectively a source of security for African women. A major cause of poverty is the dominance of women-headed households in many black communities, given the difficulty for black women to find reasonably paid employment. In factory work, the labour force remains very heavily male and the most notable trend in hiring women comes in areas removed from the cities where the cheapness of immobile local female labour is at a premium. Relatively few black, as opposed to white or brown, women, are trained or hired for office work still and the majority labour in the fields or as domestics, and thus are peripheral to industrial production in South Africa.

Even the cheapest of house designs that appear available for the working class in South Africa are beyond the means of the majority at the present. What falls below that level are only the site-and-service schemes that do not provide a modicum of reasonable amenities for inhabitants although they may seem tolerable for impoverished migrants. A huge indeterminate proportion of township dwellers ceased paying rent in the middle 1980s in response to major rent hikes that are intended to pay for the new black municipal officialdom and the services it is to control. Thus plans for substantially upgrading the conditions in which most black dwellers live seem Utopian at present.

South African state reforms seem incapable of providing any effective political base on which a new kind of politically defined black working class could emerge. Reform is limited by the imperative of avoiding political change that will delegitimate the state. The dominant forces in business as well as the bureaucracy oppose the straightforward granting of majority rule, which would inevitably bring African nationalism to the fore in some form and marginalise the dominant white political forces of the present. Reform is thus presented as a purely technocratic exercise dependent for its transmission and enactment on loyal black officials who lack credibility and power and fail to give it any kind of social vitality.

Educational reform, for instance, advocates increased spending on black education and ultimately an equalization of education for all 'races' under segregated conditions; there is within it a particular emphasis on functional improvements and technical training. As the schools expand, with second-rate or worse facilities, the lack of consensual power structures and more attractive cultural and political ideas to accompany any upgrading becomes very manifest. Educational growth has in fact led to boycotts, destruction and closures of schools. There is a widening gulf between colour-blind, technocratic views expressed by the reforming De Lange Commission and the people's education movement which has won the day amongst black pupils. This is a telling example of the heightening of social and economic tension through the pursuit of reforms directed exclusively from the top.

Trade unions organising black workers must steer their way through this storm. Trade unions were introduced to South Africa in the nineteenth century by immigrant artisans who were most effective when their organisations revolved around the preservation of genuine work skills. Protection of workers often took the form of a colour bar, so that race came often to coincide with skill level and, in a sense, helped to cement the boundaries within the working class. Simultaneously other unions turned to more incorporative structures and tried to bring workers of all colours into their organisations. Such unions generally contained a strongly paternalistic flavour with white officials in an unquestioned position of dominance. Until the early 1920s relations between white bosses and white workers were often stormy but thereafter, as the white working class became more prosperous and more involved with supervision, militancy declined, strikes became rare and the trade unions often degenerated into benefit societies. The most committed trade unionists broke with this tradition from the second decade of the twentieth century to try and organise black unskilled workers. In the aftermath of World War I, a first significant wave of black worker strikes occurred, notably on the gold mines.

This period is most associated with the rise and fall of the Industrial and Commercial Workers Union which arose in

1919 and claimed up to 100,000 members at its peak in the following decade. Within the ICU's most dynamic decade, historians can observe at once reformist tendencies, Communist Party infiltration and attempts to create a well-articulated and industrially organised trade-union movement on the model of Britain. It was a platform for the ambitions of a leadership, notably that of the Nyasalander Clements Kadalie, from outside the working class and it functioned, particularly in rural areas, as a messianic nationalist movement that made demands unrealisable outside of a political revolution. Eventually the failure to achieve anything concrete and the tugging from all sides brought about collapse by the end of the 1920s. The ICU's history represents a first stage in the political development of African workers.

It is possible to see the history of black worker organisation as one of waves that assumed considerable scope and impact but then crashed back leaving little organisational trace. This was true of the ICU. A second wave was that associated with the Congress of Non-European Trade Unions (CNETU) focussed on consumer goods industries which quickly achieved a large membership during World War II when jobs were available and black workers in a strong bargaining position. The state, moreover, was experimenting with a more liberal labour policy and not averse to improving wages in more productive factories. CNETU dissolved in the years following the defeat of a major miners' strike in 1946. A third wave is associated with the South African Congress of Trade Unions (SACTU), which formed when the old Trade and Labour Congress dissolved in 1955, its old ambiguity about simultaneously maintaining white privilege and the need to organise unskilled, black workers becoming impossible to sustain. SACTU, the radical wing with much of the black membership, linked itself closely to the African National Congress and the underground Communist Party, and was as much an attempt to use workers as a political arm in a nationalist struggle as an effective association of worker organisations. In the wake of the banning of the ANC and its turn to armed struggle, SACTU, although never made illegal, was effectively crushed with many of its organisers gaoled or exiled and most of its component unions died out.

What appears to be at this writing a far more stable trade-union movement now functioning is very recent in origin. Its roots are diverse. The Trade Union Congress of South Africa (TUCSA), the more conservative spin-off from the Trade and Labour Congress as compared to SACTU, sponsored so-called 'parallel' unions for 'non-whites'. The massification of industry and the growing maturity of a working class among a few groups such as the Coloured carworkers of the eastern Cape led to increasing unrest in these 'parallel' unions dissatisfied with TUCSA paternalism and co-operation with the state. Secondly, the city-wide Durban strikes, initiated in the textile industry in 1973 virtually without any leadership or outside influence, inspired a key group of largely white students and intellectuals to commit themselves to organising a new trade-union movement. Thirdly, SACTU veterans such as Harry Gwala in the Pietermaritzburg area, arguably played a significant role in some places in reviving union organisation. Until the Wiehahn Commission of 1979, the new trade unions struggled and were only able to survive state repression and to organise with difficulty. Then came a dramatic turn-around. The state decided to permit the registration of non-racial trade unions and to legalise strikes. Those unions that decided for strategic reasons to accept registration formed the Federation of South African Trade Unions (FOSATU). Thereafter in the 1980s, the new unions were able to expand very dramatically in membership and in their capacity to organise, particularly in secondary industry, but also from about 1983 on the mines. At first battles were largely over the creation of less authoritarian labour practices. The practical successes of the new unions have been significant. However with time, some categories of workers have experienced improved wages and benefits. Issues such as health and safety or, far more tentatively, sex discrimination have begun to be taken up. The most important shift, however, has been towards a recognition of worker rights. In the early 1980s, it is indicative that many industrial struggles were against dismissals of workers or in response to provocation by harsh or racist supervision. With the emphasis in many unions on creating shop-steward structures and internal democracy, workers acquired a new experience of managing their own affairs, fighting their own struggles and achieving a sense of self-confidence in an industrial milieu thus cutting through the historic dependence on workplace control through gang-leaders, treated as substitute chiefs, and company informers.

Most of the new trade union movement, from FOSATU and elsewhere, came together in 1985 into the Congress of South African Trade Unions (COSATU) a federation that then represented 565,000 workers and continued to emphasise workplace organisation and class issues while avoiding bureaucratisation or undue power accruing to the leadership. As a result, real power resides in the big industrial affiliates, not the congress. Within COSATU there are intense debates about the role trade unions ought to play politically and as to their engagement in struggles against the state. There is as well the Council of Unions of South Africa which has rejected the 'non-racialism' of COSATU for a more exclusively black nationalist position on politics. CUSA is a far smaller (and less consistently militant) federation than COSATU since the desertion of the National Union of Mineworkers. There are other trade unions organising black workers as well in South Africa; apolitical

TUCSA dissolved in 1986 but its principal components, now independent, mainly organise Indian, Coloured and African workers.

COSATU shares the ideal of non-racialism with the exiled Congress movement. Concretely this is symbolised by the important role that has been played by white organisers and other trade-union workers in many of the COSATU components. However, it is equally important to note that COSATU unions include disproportionately few Coloured, very few Indian and virtually no white workers. Not only are the COSATU unions on the whole geared towards unskilled and operative labour but they are fuelled by a social movement that is part of, and indeed fundamental to, the growing politicisation of African urban life, particularly perhaps in the industrial heartland of the southern Transvaal. TUCSA was a union federation that reflected far better the different racial elements in society as a whole, dominated by an old white leadership and either avoiding politics or giving some support to state reform policies. The growing political divide between black workers and others was a major reason for its collapse just as greater shopfloor militancy within TUCSA proved unsustainable divorced from the political movement within the black working class.

Most scholars who have examined grassroots politics in tropical Africa have remarked on the depth of resentment of the rich and privileged among poor people while noting that this fails to develop into a consistent class-based politics of the type found in many parts of the world. An obvious reason for this is the relatively light weight of the industrial proletariat in the economy even of the more developed countries as Kenya, Zimbabwe, Nigeria or Ghana. In the case of South Africa, this is obviously much less true. The South African worker is not a drop in the ocean nor is he or she suffused by a world of petty commerce and production that permits people to see their future in getting out of the working class. Thus surveys of South African township dwellers' grievances pick up problems that are common to all working-class populations: housing, transport, social amenities, education, consumer crises of all sorts. One might consequently expect the development of socialist politics within the black working class.

Working against this are a number of counter-factors. There remains a weighty population outside the industrial proletariat, which in accordance with an economic down-turn and with international trends is growing amongst those who are black and poor. The creation of a working class cut off from rural values and possibilities is a relatively new phenomenon for blacks running back only one or perhaps two generations in most families. It is a working class that has emerged in an industrial environment weak for various reasons in artisanal skills and poorly educated beyond a limited literacy (or, cut off from the white 'labour aristocracy' far stronger here). As yet there is only the beginnings of a political culture infused with a sense of its place in the world.

However, the principal reason for the weakness of a distinctive workers' politics is the continued, indeed re-newed, strength of a populist–nationalist tradition effec-tively dominated by the African National Congress which is historically not very different from equivalent political movements in tropical Africa (ZAPU and ZANU in Zimbabwe, UNIP in Zambia, KANU in Kenya). That tra-dition has an essentially colonial resonance. Although lacking any coherent theory of social transition, it contains the vision of a world turned upside down where the South Africa that has been largely shaped by the demands and struggles of the different classes within *white* society would be remade into a returned and renewed 'Africa'.

The ANC does contain certain elements which mark it

off from conventional African nationalist movements. Apart from the nominal claims about the working class as the vanguard of the struggle, there is the historic alliance with the Communist Party, which has always emphasised the importance of trade unions and made claims about the potential pre-eminence of class politics (without any corresponding effective mass organisation, be it said). There is as well a civil-rights aspect to the ANC thrust which consequently contains, as well through the emphasis on non-racialism, the germs of a democratic critique of existing South African society that has an intellectual power attractive to workers. Within COSATU, the leadership, probably reflecting the views of most black workers, has for now accepted the centrality of the 'national democratic' struggle led by the ANC and its allies, leaving social transformation to a secondary and vaguer stage. At the same time, there are numerous tendencies in the unions that increasingly debate how to make that struggle relevant to workers, how to advocate a future that will avoid the destruction of independent trade unions at the hands of an unsteady and authoritarian state as elsewhere in Africa. Some circles raise the issues of workers' control and the transition to socialism. Thus while black working-class politics, perhaps because of the power of nationalist politics on the imagination in a society dominated by the alienating counter-nationalism of a minority, is yet unable to envision a distinct socialist party based on its own concerns, the nationalist movement itself is forced to consider issues and debates that push it more in a class-orientated direction than the analogy with countries north of the Limpopo might suggest. Finally, the fluidity of the situation at the time of writing must be stressed; the issues raised are unsettled.

What would the situation of labour be in a post-apartheid South Africa? Superficially it looks at first as though there must be every likelihood of a strongly labour-orientated regime that would rectify the restrictions that have crippled the material well-being and cultural growth of black workers in the existing order of things. However, the structuring of the South African economy in the course of industrialisation presents some formidable problems that could not be undone easily. Proletarianised South Africans, cut off from the land, are now to be found in very large numbers in partially urban settlements that are remote from cities and from convenient sources of employment. The desegregation of housing, even the construction of new public housing on a big scale, will not quickly solve their problems. The white-owned farms continue to contain a large surplus of impoverished workers while the survival of migrant labour suggests another set of dilemmas. Should the state bring jobs to where the people are or bring the people to the jobs? What means are there, given the attrition of petty production and the level of concentration in the economy, for stimulating the massive creation of jobs and sophisticated skills? How can legislation cope with the particular problems of women who cannot be slotted into the social welfare structures modelled on the Western nuclear family? Although the trade-union movement is beginning to think beyond the workplace and to form alliances with social forces that might be the germ of a long-term solution to such problems, the development of coherent policies is still virtually beyond the horizon. The really deprived in South African society are in any case not the most militant and best-organised workers.

Some of the current thinking about 'post-apartheid' society comes rather too easy. It is not clear at all what sort of economy such a society would inherit, for instance after a relatively long and effective sanctions campaign that might have devastated or attenuated many parts of industry. There is also the sobering issue of potential war conditions and the departure of people with vital skills. At the same time, the staying power of the South African system and the white nationalism that has been so far the politically dominant feature should not be underestimated. 'Post-apartheid' society might represent a deal struck preserving many existing features. It is still by no means certain that black nationalism in South Africa has the wherewithal short of massive foreign intervention even to achieve such a deal! While we have identified various constraints that make it very difficult to see the African worker in most of the continent achieve political coherence or form the political basis at present for a transition to a radically different sort of society, South Africa, even though it suffers very much less from such constraints, embodies a particular and distinctive set of challenges to organised workers and to those engaged in the humane transformation of the world of labour.

7

LABOUR, THE
DEVELOPMENT PROCESS
AND SOCIAL CHANGE

In much of the contemporary literature on Africa, there is a remarkable gulf between discussions of economic development both prescriptive and descriptive, and the literature which forms the basis for this book on labour. When development is the subject, attention is primarily given to questions of technology, infrastructure, finance and terms of trade. In the typical colonial literature, the prime emphasis lay on getting the native to work under the most desirable conditions for capital or the state. Now in part because it is no longer so clear from the point of various managerial imperatives how to motivate that labour in the most appropriate way, labour has disappeared from much of the debates on development. Although W. Arthur Lewis as ideological progenitor of African development economics gave fundamental weight to improving the skill and increasing the scarcity and bargaining power of African workers (Lewis, 1954), manpower studies are not very central to development economics as they have progressed over the past quarter-century.

One crucial way of coming to grips with labour and its social as well as economic context, is through the framework of class. The introduction of the idea of class into studies of African labour has provided a far more lucid approach than colonial managerial strictures. However, despite the advantage of class as a paradigm, the Marxist road into capitalism via outright proletarianisation in tropical Africa provides only limited satisfaction. For one thing, Africans have been surprisingly successful in prolonging their resistance to proletarianisation, thus qualifying the class character of their early development as wage workers. For another, the economic development of Africa since independence has too clearly faltered from the point of view of absorption of an industrialised population committed to a mass-production economy.

The reality is a painful one. African states do not have the wherewithal to sustain industrialisation, still dependent on foreign aid, technology, spare parts and raw materials. Their own agricultural and mineral exports have declined in international purchasing power, if not actually absolute value and quantity. It is not conceivable that Africans will simply cheerfully retreat back to the subsistence economy. The range of new needs, the dependence on exchange, the transformation of household and family structures has gone too far even in out of the way regions. Johan Pottier has recently made a study of the Mambwe villagers in northern Zambia that Watson considered almost thirty years earlier (Pottier, 1983). No longer is there a convenient articulation between migrant-based cash earnings and a functioning rural subsistence base. With the decline of the copper mine labour force and the generalisation of an urban-bred working population, migrant opportunities have drastically declined in Zambia and elsewhere. This is true even in South Africa now. Yet people consider cash-acquired goods and services fundamental. Mambwe villages contain few sources for earning cash nor are they geared effectively to subsistence. The Mambwe situation has deteriorated very substantially. 'People now survive from "raiding" the socialist economy . . . contraband commerce and intensified petty trading . . . The former low-cost industrial reserve has turned itself, at the height of a nationwide economic crisis, into a no-cost redistribution unit' (Pottier, 1983, 15–17). This kind of re-structuring accompanied by intensifying poverty is reported from many different areas, for instance by Jette Bukh, with regard to the position of women, in the once-thriving cocoa bush of southern Ghana, now again an area at once dependent on and starved for cash (Bukh, 1979).

With the increasing scarcity of imports, it is possible for local forms of production and interchange to expand. This is partially a healthy response away from the extraverted character of the 'dependent' economy of the late colonial period but it must be seen in the context of new class relations and forms of exploitation that will be of increasing importance in the evolution of labour conditions. It lies at the heart of the rise of the 'informal sector', which is a window to the characteristic class structures that sustain African capitalism. Those structures threaten the future prospects of those workers who are involved in systematic waged or salaried work for the state or larger-scale enterprise and whose capacity for organisation is so much greater, unless they possess scarce skills.

Two related conventional responses to development needs, both of them problematic, have acted on this deteriorating scenario. One is the authoritarian imperative, already encountered in some of these pages. Only the state (or multi-nationals, acting in conjunction with the state) can reach out to seize control of much of the labour and the product of the mass of the population effectively, it proposes. Discipline can harness labour, and in time a development breakthrough under paternalist auspices can take place. A particularly disastrous example has been the easy assumption made in purportedly radical states that the backwardness of peasant farming, as measured in terms of low productivity, can readily be eliminated through the institution of state farms which could provide convenient funnels for large injections of capital as well as savings of scale and more scientific management. In practice, state farms have worked poorly, notably in Angola and Mozambique most recently, for lack of any serious consultation with the peasantry, any sense of the relevant labour process and its many constraints and out of a faulty conception of what state initiatives can accomplish. Peasants can easily slip out of their unwanted obligations. This approach has led to a silent but enervating war with the peasantry and the decline or collapse of production.

The second response, not unrelated, is to bypass the human factor and rely on technology to do the trick in creating economic forward leaps. Yet technology cannot work if inserted against the grain of existing social relations. Massive aid projects in rural Nigeria to create 'master' farmers and boost capitalist farming go to ground for lack of a suitable rural workforce. In much of Africa, development training and aid is directed to men when the actual relevant work is largely done by women who do not, however, have much obvious power in the society. These approaches are not only oppressive and divisive, they also generally fail in their own productionist terms.

It may be suggested that where development actually occurs effectively (and the past decade has made all thinking observers far more sceptical of the potential of structured managerial input of all sorts in the African context), it will be because it harnesses the creative skill potential of workers of all sorts, rural as well as urban, female as well as male. The particular character of relations between men and women and the particular advantages and disadvantages of migration are among the many factors that need to be considered in the evolution of an effective labour force that maximises the human possibilities currently available. The diffusion of skills that mark the ability to master late twentieth-century economic forms must somehow come to fit an amplification of skills and knowledge available as part of the long adaptation of Africans to their native environment. In any coherent movement out of underdevelopment, the effective use of African labour will be essential. The colonial assessment, whatever its other failings, was perfectly correct here.

South Africa presents the one exception where an industrial economy has developed. However, the South African worker faces a particularly difficult, if different, set of problems before political and social constraints of contemporary South African development can be overcome and the majority of workers acquire the education, rights and self-confidence hitherto confined largely to whites. Nonetheless the potential for an integrated development centred on South Africa, were it to become politically feasible, clearly presents one of the few more obviously hopeful possibilities, at least for an important corner of Africa. This is largely because of the level of skill, organisation and coherence which can be found in the South African labour force following the course of its tumultuous and struggle-filled history.

Beyond this, the battle for a better way of life for the mass of Africans which should be at the core of the development process, is apt to be a long one. The material, cultural and social formation of the African worker is going to be central to it.

✿ 8 ✿

A GUIDE TO THE
LITERATURE ON LABOUR IN
AFRICA

The purpose of this chapter is to present in readable form an introduction to those books and other written work that seem particularly useful for exploring the themes of this study. To some extent the structure of the preceding chapters will be followed but it appears desirable to cluster work around the subjects that have attracted particularly rich bibliographical attention in recent years and thus this chapter has its own means of proceeding that is defined by the sub-headings that divide it. Amongst more detailed and comprehensive bibliographic guides to the subject, readers may find useful Martens (1977) and Orimalade (1974). The literature in French is highlighted in Copans (1981). The bibliographic sections in the *Review of African Political Economy* (*ROAPE*) have been most helpful.

GENERAL WORKS AND MAIN THEMES

It has been suggested in chapter 1 that a few paradigmatic works can bring together very well the principal ideas of recent literature on labour in Africa. The promotion of a flexible idea of class analysis of African society that is central to Sandbrook and Cohen (1975) and the historical range available in Gutkind, Cohen and Copans (1979) give this significance to them in particular. Robin Cohen has been a central figure in pioneering a new approach to labour studies and synthesising ideas (Cohen, 1976, 1980) as has Peter Gutkind (1974). Even at this early stage, it seems important to emphasise the work of Charles van Onselen who really put labour history on the African scholarly map (van Onselen, 1976) as well as a critical article which seems to sum up the problems that many social scientists have had with his perspective (Goldberg, 1981).

Class analysis in turn leads us back to the suggestive if rigid political Marxism of an earlier era. Thus Cohen found the work of Albert Nzula done in Moscow at the beginning of the 1930s very interesting (Nzula, Potekhin and Zusmanovich, 1979). Other literature deriving from this tradition includes Sik (1966–74) and Woddis (1959). For an interpretation of Sik, see Bernstein (1977). In moving towards issues around which the most contentious material on African labour has been produced, the assessment of African trade unions and their political significance by Berg and Butler remains stimulating (1964). The subsequent debate on the meaning of post-independence worker activity in Nigeria opened up the questions which have been central to research in the past ten to fifteen years (Berg, 1969; Weeks, 1968, 1971a, 1971b; Kilby, 1967, 1968; Warren, 1966, 1969; Cohen, 1971).

One important section of Left literature had been suspicious of the social impact of the organised working class in late colonial and independent Africa and was inclined to talk in terms of an African labour aristocracy (Arrighi, 1970 but also from a politically less committed perspective, Bates, 1971 and Drake and Lacey, 1966). See as well Amsden, 1971 for a more nuanced approach. Such a point of view can also be found in polemical form in Fanon (1963). For early defenders of the African organised working class, see Braundi and Lettieri (1964) and Guérin (1964) who concern themselves respectively with the Nigerian General Strike and the Ghanaian labour movement in conflict with

Nkrumah. During the 1970s, the whole idea of an African labour aristocracy came under attack as part of the project of considering an African working class as historical actor (Jeffries, 1975; Hinchliffe, 1974; Waterman, 1975). Some have interpreted Fanon as privileging the 'lumpen-proletariat' with a special revolutionary class character; this was subjected to criticism by Cohen and Michael (1976).

Those who argued for the taming of a labour aristocracy were still generally impressed by the militancy of peasant, or semi-peasant, migrants into the wage labour force. Some formulations of this question include Allen's classic definition of the peasantry as a sort of proletariat (V. Allen, 1972) and a systematic economic study of rural and urban relations amongst workers in Senegal (Lakroum, 1983). For some, migration has appeared as the central feature in a distinctively African form of capital accumulation (Rey, 1976) while others have defended a more typical process of proletarianisation with migration as more of a short-term historical phase (Cohen, 1976). Some contemporary studies of labour migration from the most varied standpoints include Amin (1974), Amselle (1976), Chrétien (1978), Clarke (1974a), Diop (1965), Elkan (1980), Freund (1981b), Newbury (1975), Parkin (1976), Pottier (1983), Sabot (1979), Sender (1974), Stichter (1985). Other work on migrancy is referred to below in the context of historical or country-specific sources and elsewhere.

HISTORICAL WORK: PRE-COLONIAL AND AFTER

Labour has become a significant theme in the study of pre-conquest Africa, largely by the way of considerations of the idea of using the Marxist method of presenting historical eras as modes of production. See Coquery-Vidrovitch and Suret-Canale in Suret-Canale (1974) for the evolution of this approach (also *Canadian Journal of African Studies*, 1985).

With this focus on the cultivator, Meillassoux (1972, 1981) provides an arresting and widely considered model in highly abstracted form. Pierre-Philippe Rey offers theoretical amplification (Rey, 1976) while Emmanuel Terray attempted one important historical case study (1974). Raymond Dumett has invoked scepticism, however, on whether Terray's picture is historically accurate (Dumett, 1979). The strengths and weaknesses of mode of production research come forward in a useful collection by Stewart and Crummey (1981) and one can turn as well to other studies in Vidal (1974) and Clarence-Smith (1979a).

Many historians agree on the widespread importance for labour history, amongst other areas of interest, of the institution of slavery and related forms of coercive control over people in pre-conquest Africa. Among those studies of slavery that are most helpful to the understanding of how labour underpinned a variety of pre-colonial African economies, see Meillassoux, ed. (1975); Cooper (1977, 1979); Lovejoy (1979, 1983). Diop (1981) contains a remarkable attempt to decode the 'caste' system of western West Africa. Several studies, generally also on West Africa, have explored labour relations in pre-conquest commodity production involving free as well as slave labour (Alpers in Coquery-Vidrovitch, 1983; Jaggar, 1973; Shea, 1975).

HISTORICAL WORK: COLONIAL

The shift towards growing commodification of social relations was part of an upheaval which helped to cause and partially accompanied the Scramble for Africa. The relationship of this to the attack on the slave trade, actual expansion of slaving and slavery as an institution and then its final decline have been particularly interesting for historians. Among those studies that are especially useful for a labour historian must be ranked Clarence-Smith (1979b),

Coquery-Vidrovitch (1971); Cooper (1981a); Duffy (1967); Iliffe (1980) and Weiskel (1979).

Colonial literature on African labour made it a central theme. The two most important issues were the question of coercion and that of stabilisation of the workforce and arguments were made on both sides particularly before World War II. On the whole, it was considered desirable to preserve African labour on the land to avoid the social costs and conflicts that a full-scale proletarianisation would bring. Coercion was also seen as partially counter-productive. Nonetheless no writer who would be taken seriously within the colonial world would reject the fundamental need for pursuing capital accumulation in the interests of the colonising country. A sampling of this literature would include Olivier (1929); Lugard (1929); Ninine (1932); Orde Brown (1932) and the survey by an American critic sympathetic to liberal colonialism as it was then defined, Buell (1928). For excellent analytical considerations of colonial labour policy with value for readers from the entire continent, see Iliffe (1980) and Lonsdale and Berman (1979, 1980).

There is quite a sharp shift in the landscape and in the relevant literature after World War II. A useful introduction to the new context is Low and Lonsdale (1976). Landmark works explaining the thrust of economic development as deliberate state policy are Lewis (1954) and Myint (1965). For some general assessments within a policy outlook that take up the issues of proletarianisation and trade unionism in the various colonial systems, see Powesland (1957); Richards (1952); Wilson and Wilson (1945); Mendes (1958); Murteira (1960); Lux (1962, and thus continuing into the independence era); Doucy and Feldheim (1952); Périn-Hockers (1959); Doucy (1954); *Estudo sobre o absentismo* . . . (1960). These themes were particularly extended into a more scholarly and less colonially committed wider audience by Balandier (1952); Naville (1952); Roper (1958) and Hodgkin (1956), still a useful book that yields many insights.

A special amount of attention was devoted to reconsidering the problem of labour migration which was both expanding in scale but breaking down as a coherent system as the permanent urban population grew in the 1940s and the 1950s. Migration and stabilisation were the backbone issues of the important scholarly research promoted in Northern Rhodesia (now Zambia), for which see especially Wilson (1941), Epstein (1958) and Mitchell (1956; 1961a; 1961b; 1969) and they were subjected to a harsh but important critique by Magubane (1971). However the subject found many other considerations including those in Read (1942); Schapera (1947); Gulliver (1955); Prothero (1957); Watson (1958); van Velsen (1960); Skinner (1960); Rouch (1956) and Elkan (1960 and 1976). For a closely related study on independent Liberia, see Fraenkel (1964) and for 'detribalisation' and urbanisation in South Africa, Hellman (1948) and Glass (1960). The contrasting approach to migration from Mozambique to South Africa and the Rhodesias is striking in Harris (1959) and Rita Ferreira (1960; 1963).

Another area opened up with numerous publications concerning the new trade unions. Davies (1966) is still an interesting assessment in some respects. For others, extending into the post-colonial years, see Beling (1968); Meynaud and Salah-Bey (1962); Ndiaye (1964) and November (1965) while the industrial relations/collective bargaining structures enter African studies with Yesufu (1962); Roberts and de Bellecombe (1967) and Bokonga (1967). Historians of colonial Africa have provided us with a large amount of material that considers the issues about which debates raged in detail and from the point of view of the economy as a whole and sometimes of the colonial labouring population as well. In particular, much work has been done on structures of colonial political economy. The developmental ideas of Myint and W.A. Lewis, amongst others, have received some knocks through debates that are taken up in Berg (1961); Fetter and Miracle (1970); Hogendorn (1976); Freund and Shenton (1977) and Tosh (1978). Organising an exploration of the more specific literature, however, is best taken up regionally.

For West Africa, one might start with Robin Cohen's useful survey on Nigerian labour (1976) which does touch on colonial issues and development to an important extent although much of its focus lies in the post-colonial period. Other historical work on Nigerian labour and outside collections referred to above should mention Hopkins (1966); Mason in Gutkind et al. (1979); Akpala (1965); Oyemakinde (1974b); Osoba (1969); Shenton (1986) and Freund (1981a and 1982). Conway surveyed labour in Sierra Leone as 'protest activity' (Conway, 1968) while Richard Joseph did the same in a particular conjuncture for Cameroon (1974). Forced labour in the 1920s forms the heart of an important article by Roger Thomas (1973) on the Gold Coast as well as work on the colonial history of French Africa: Babassana (1978); Anouma (1976); Fall (1976/77 and 1983) and Sautter (1967). Apart from Lakroum's general reconsideration of labour supply in colonial Senegal, there are also some useful articles on the history of organised labour there: Suret-Canale in Gutkind et al. (1979); Thiam (1976); Bernard-Duguenet (1977) and Ndour (1981). Particularly salient to the history of labour in the Belgian Congo are Tshibangu (1974); Demunter (1972) and Jewsiewicki et al. (1973), all concerned with coercion and resistance.

Bruce Fetter has written about the Katanga copper mines (1973) as a totalitarian society. By contrast, see Charles Perrings' comparative book on Katanga and the Copper Belt of Northern Rhodesia (1979). The Copper Belt with its remarkable history of labour organisation and proletarianisation has attracted other historians as well, amongst which are: Perrings (1977); Parpart (1983); Berger (1974) and Henderson (1973a; 1973b; 1974). Colonial Southern Rhodesia with its important history of a working class structured by manufacturing and wage labour in agriculture as well as mining has attracted the interest of Arrighi (1973); van Onselen (1976); Makenzie (1970); Phimister (1977); Phimister and van Onselen (1976); Moyo (1973) and Malaba (1980). Malawi's situation in the colonial labour markets is the subject of Sanderson (1961). Mozambique has been equally important as an exporter of labour but Penvenne has written interestingly about the history of workers in Maputo (Penvenne 1979a and 1979b). Vail and White have produced a major study that considers not only many aspects of the history of proletarianisation and labour in northern Mozambique but also the emergence of a sub-continental labour system and its implications (Vail and White, 1980). For South West Africa, see Moorsom (1977; 1979). The former British East African colonies, especially Kenya, have also been interesting to historians of labour. Clayton and Savage have written a long general account focussing on state policy in Kenya (Clayton and Savage, 1974) while Stichter has written about migration, women workers and politics particularly (Stichter, 1975, 1982a, 1982b). Labour in the context of political economy dominates van Zwanenberg (1975). Fred Cooper considers class formation, worker life and politics and colonial reaction in an historical study of Mombasa (Cooper, 1987). For Mombasa labour history, see as well Janmohamed (1976). The Sudanese labour system as part of an articulated colonial political economy is laid out provocatively by O'Brien (1983), who, in so doing, summarises considerable local scholarship while an introduction to the organised labour movement as it looked at the time of independence is available in Fawzi (1957). Snyder (1981) considers the central agency of colonial law in shaping the new working class of colonial Africa. Obviously many of the other works highlighted in other sections of this chapter also contain an historical dimension that supplements these works.

TRADE UNIONS

Much of the literature most accessible on African trade unions is historical and the distinction between this section and its predecessor is not a hard and fast one. Nonetheless it seems useful to distinguish between historical work on labour in general and trade-union research apt to have a more contemporary component. Reference has already been made to the body of literature from the 1950s and 1960s that tried to come to grips from a managerial perspective with the growing organisation of labour in Africa; amongst works taking the part of labour, Hodgkin (1956) and Woddis (1959) deserve a second mention. Davies (1966) still reads quite usefully and serves as an introduction to its theme. Damachi et al. (1979) is a more contemporary introduction. Ananaba (1979) is a partisan account from the perspective of Cold War rivalries but interesting. See also Geiss (1965) and the bibliographic essay by Friedland (1974).

The trade-union literature on Nigeria is quite well-developed. A logical first step into it is Cohen (1974) followed by the analysis of a prominent official in Ananaba (1969). Among those who, like him, discuss the General Strike of 1964 are Braundi and Lettieri (1964); Melson (1970) and Oyemakinde (1974a). Melson (1973) and Waterman (1973) from very different points of view talk about the political situation of organised Nigerian labour. See also the literature that was situated around the debate that resulted in a critique of the Berg–Butler thesis above, including Warren (1966). There is a revealing portrait of a trade union in the First Republic era available in Smock (1969). During the

1970s, Nigerian trade-union studies are well-represented in the Sandbrook and Cohen collection, notably in contributions by Remy and Lubeck. No organised group of workers has been as intensely studied as the dock and portworkers of Lagos as a result of the labours of Peter Waterman. For principal themes, see Waterman (1977 and 1978). So far the organisational changes and struggles ensuing from the growing attempts by the Nigerian state to establish structural control over the union has attracted a substantial polemical literature but little considered or detailed study.

The confrontation between a substantial part of organised labour and the Nkrumah regime attracted a number of scholars to a consideration of the labour movement in Ghana. It is even possible to locate a locally derived literature from within its ranks (Tettegah, 1962, for instance). There are some interesting assessments of the political spectrum in Trachtman (1962); Cowan (1961); Drake and Lacey (1966); Gerritsen (1972); Damachi (1974); Crisp (1978); Gray (1981) and especially Kraus (1979). Stimulating introductions to the trade-union movements in other West African countries include Mayson and Sawyer on Liberia (1979) and C. Allen on the Gambia (1970). Warmington's detailed study of plantation worker organisation in British Cameroons was published at the end of the colonial era (1960). Pfefferman has written on unions for the whole of colonial French West Africa (1967) as well as a more substantial study of Senegal alone. For the development of Senegalese trade unionism from perspectives sympathetic to a class analysis, see Mulot (1979); Ndour (1981); Bernard-Duguenet (1977) and Rita Cruise O'Brien (1979). On other French-speaking countries, Bonis (1973) is fascinating and Brabcova-Chelli (1977) helpful.

Zambian miners have been the subject of many important studies, so much so that their salience to trade-union accounts is only one aspect of the literature. References exist elsewhere to the writings of Bates, Burawoy and

Epstein, Henderson and Parpart because their arguments are so important to the general issues raised in this book or because they are crucial for the history of labour in Zambia. Discussions of the position of organised labour in pre-1980 Rhodesia are found in Ranger (1970), Brand (1971) and Harris (1975).

Another country marked by tension between trade unions and the post-colonial state was Tanzania. This history is best introduced through Friedland (1967; 1969). When factory workers in Dar es Salaam succeeded in mounting a strike wave with a Left political ambiance quite outside the orbit of the state-controlled unions, a number of sympathetic analysts took up their initiative: Mihyo (1975), Mapolu (1976) and Shivji (1976). On the labour context in Tanzania during the 1970s, see as well D. Jackson (1979) and Kjekshus (1977). A solid account of trade unions in Uganda early in the independence era is available from Scott (1966). We have as well very careful and important research on the Kampala railway workers by Ralph Grillo (1973 and 1974).

Writers on labour in Kenya such as Clayton and Savage, Cooper and Stichter have much to say about trade unions. There are surveys of the situation of the unions and their relation to the state and capital in Amsden (1971) and in Leitner (1972) from radical perspectives critical of trade unionism, and a memoir from an important unionist of the late colonial era in the guise of a history, Singh (1969). Richard Sandbrook has written a more complex study of the unions that goes beyond the more general material and challenges some stereotypes (Sandbrook, 1972 and 1975).

WORKPLACE AND COMMUNITY

A major underlying thrust of this book is its recognition of the importance of moving beyond institutional studies in order to understand not merely the character of trade unions in Africa but also to come to a deeper understanding of the politics of labour and class in the African context. This section emphasises those studies that have gone particularly beyond the traditional boundaries of labour studies but is by no means irrelevant to or entirely separated from the work that is surveyed in the last section. Some provocative or evocative work that has in a general way tried to characterise the political views and class perspective of workers in Africa would be Williams (1974); Gutkind (1975); Sandbrook (1977); Sandbrook and Arn (1977); Waterman (1976) all of whom are trying to come to grips with a West African populist consciousness. This is true in a different way of the historical writing of Frank Furedi on Nairobi (1973).

The writing of Michael Burawoy on Zambian copper mines is characterised by the force of his critique of economic, statist and overly institutional analyses and his ambitious and interesting attempts to understand consciousness through actual studies of human relations at the workplace (Burawoy, 1972a, 1972b, 1982). *The Politics of Production* extends this into a comparative framework for industry internationally (Burawoy, 1985). There are some interesting studies situated in Africa which use a number of eclectic frameworks for understanding what goes on at the workplace, notably Gordon (1977); Alverson (1978); Kapferer (1972 and the more successful study in 1976); Moodie (in Bozzoli, 1983) and Bonis (1973).

The harsh and politically sometimes contradictory world of gold miners in Ghana has been contextualised by two Marxist writers: Jim Silver (1978, 1981) and Jeff Crisp (1979, 1984). From Leger (1985) much can be grasped of the labour process in South African mines today. Two fine studies of working-class life amongst communities where organised workers are prominent in West Africa are Jeffries

(1978) and Peace (1979). While Paul Lubeck is especially interested in the urban Islamic context of class militancy in Kano (Lubeck, 1978, 1979), Hinchliffe has written a solid survey of the industrial labour force in the textile mills of Kaduna (1973). For a survey of Ghanaian factories, see Peil (1970) and a 'psychosociological' assessment of Dakar workers, Hauser (1968). Sketchley and Lappe (1980) consider very positively the changing labour context in a Mozambican foundry after independence where tensions between an ideology of liberation and, by extension, workers' control and the state's needs for production are revealed.

If Sandbrook has tried to consider why Kenya has not given birth to a labour-based socialism amongst its urban workers from the standpoint of trade-union structure, other writers have emphasised instead the urban context itself to discuss local politics, patronage and class alliances in the poor quarters of urban East Africa (Bujra, 1978/79, Chege, 1981). Bruce Fetter has written a monograph on Zairois urban history that situates the living space of Katanga copper miners in part (1976). Urban, and by extension working-class, culture is really the subject of Ranger, 1975. These studies can be most profitably read in conjunction both with more narrowly-focussed union studies, historical work or the material touched on below that extends the conventional definition of labour studies entirely.

LABOUR IN AGRICULTURE

For the reader who seeks a general introduction into the conditions under which cultivation takes place in tropical Africa with a strong ecological referent, Allan (1965) remains useful, if very limited on social context. The focus on labour is sharper in Cleave (1974).

There exists a very different sort of debate about the

nature of the African peasantry and its relations to capital. While V. Allen saw the peasantry as Africa's proletariat (1972), Post likes to speak of a process of 'peasantisation' with a peasantry forming in response to capital penetration (1977) and Bernstein considers a complex relationship of subordination (1977 and 1981). For those who seek to emphasise subordination, the development of an underdevelopment hypothesis is very arresting and this kind of approach with regard to Africa is best seen in Palmer and Parsons (1977). By contrast, and also for southern and south-central Africa, Ranger has emphasised continued peasant initiative (1978) while Cooper exposes the limits of a dependency approach (1981b). If numerous writers now take up historically the theme of resistance to proletarianisation amongst African peasants, there remain those who see that resistance as still largely successful (Hyden, 1980).

The phenomenon of cash crop peasant producers in Africa has attracted many writers to the most successful case studies. The best of these are growingly sensitive to the problem of labour organisation, allocation and structure for peasant producers. Two classic studies in the West African cocoa belt are Hill (1963) and Berry (1975). For other important studies: also on the Gold Coast; Robertson (1982); Bukh (1979); David on Senegal (1980); O'Brien (1983) on Sudan and Tosh (1980) on Uganda.

There is a parallel literature on plantation labour which ties in more closely to the kind of themes that emerge in studies of mining and in the history of migrant labour. The plantation theme is taken up by Clarke (1977a) and van Zwanenberg (1975) and assessed critically using South African material by Graves and Richardson (1980). Agrarian systems disposing of large-scale wage or tenant labour are at the heart of the work of Chavanduka (1972); Furedi (1976); Leitner (1976); Wilson et al. (1977) and Vail and

White (1980). Labour systems with a strong pre-capitalist feel are highlighted in Cooper (1981a) and Derman (1972) who observe their transformations.

It seems that we are having increasing success in developing a sense for how to combine the technical and ecological aspects of agrarian studies with a deeper sense for the social and historical. Ivanov is an excellent and rather well-informed Soviet survey (1979) and Swindell provides a superb general introduction, if with a bias towards West African conditions (1985). The complexities of relating the nature of labour in the countryside to the overall territorial economy have been explored for the colonial period by Lakroum (1983) and Kitching (1980). See also Vercruijsse (1979). An especially thoughtful consideration of labour in the countryside that influenced my own preparations for producing this work is Guyer (1982).

THE 'INFORMAL SECTOR'

Typical of the dubious way that economic forms that seemed out of the control of the authorities were viewed until fairly recently in the literature on Africa is Raymaekers (1963). With particular reference to the training of artisans, the centrality of the so-called informal sector to contemporary thinking on development comes out from Kenneth King's very interesting *The African Artisan* (1977). Hart's article sets the literature out provocatively and influentially (Hart, 1973). See also Senghaas-Knoblach (1977). The informal sector taken within the broader context of the urban economy is very important in Cooper (1984) and this study has made particular use of the many relevant contributions, often from a fieldwork base in Francophone Africa in Connaissance du Tiers-Monde (1983). For the ruthless suppression of squatters and unwelcome 'spontaneous' economic activity of a kind typical of tropical as much as of

South Africa, see Miti (1985). Bienefeld offers a thoughtful and grim view of artisans and traders (1975) while LeBrun and Gerry (1975) attempt to theorise the relationship of 'petty production' with capitalist accumulation more generally on the West African terrain. See de Miras (1984) here as well. For rural petty commodity production, de Jonge (1979) is interesting while Morice considers the importance of child labour (1982). For the South African literature examined critically, see Wellings and Sutcliffe (1984).

Domestic labour in Africa has been assimilated into this category to some extent. Largely neglected, the relevant literature is mainly available on South Africa notably van Onselen (1982), Cock (1980) and Gaitskell et al. (1984). However, for Rhodesia, there is Clarke (1974b) appearing during the UDI regime and for Zambia, but with suggestive material for most of tropical Africa, Hansen (1986). Also neglected but of great economic significance is the question of unemployment, but see Clarke (1977b); Hart (1976) and Parkin (1976).

WOMEN AND LABOUR

The particular characteristics of women as economic actors in Africa has always been of interest to more sensitive studies of African society and has taken on a growing importance with the impact of feminist thought. Meillassoux provides a model which classically views women as the exploited class of rural Africa (1981). This is taken up and extended by such particular studies as Henn (1982) and Jackson (1978) which see rural women as a class. A synthesis which places more weight on technology and culture but has provoked much critical interest is Boserup (1970). See as well Nelson (1981). Some studies that examine women's work on African farms raising issues about domination, poverty, co-operation and gender relations include Bukh (1979), Conti (1979), Guyer (1980a and 1980b), Hay in Hafkin and Bay (1970a) and Vaughan (1985), chosen somewhat arbitrarily from a growing literature.

The situation of women in towns, as domestic workers, as prostitutes, as wage labourers, as petty commodity producers and sellers but also as situated within a household context continues to attract a significant and interesting literature. Bryceson considers proletarianisation of women for Tanzania (1980) and Kane (1977) for Senegal. On prostitution, see particularly White in Cooper (1984). On women in the urban setting with some emphasis on economic and labour issues, particularly notable are Vidal (1977), Obbo (1980), Pittin (1984), Robertson (1984) and Oppong (1983). Stichter (1982b) and Chauncey (1981) contribute historical approaches.

Amongst the general collections that have appeared it is helpful to turn to Bay (1983), to the special issues of the *Review of African Political Economy* on women, oppression and liberation (27/28, 1984), and to the special issue of the *Journal of Southern African Studies*, 10(1), 1983. An important critical review is to be found in Bozzoli (1983).

SOUTH AFRICAN LABOUR ISSUES

The centrality of labour as a theme and a moving force within South African history and society has long been apparent and it has evoked a literature of considerable international importance. This is eloquently demonstrated for pre-war historiography by a look at de Kiewiet (1941). While no contemporary account matches de Kiewiet's success within his own liberal paradigm, current scholarship does provide a range of collections that highlight the influence of social historical research and many aspects of the way labour studies have been reconsidered. In particular, one needs to consult the rich contributional trove in Webster (1978); Marks and Atmore (1980), Marks and Rathbone (1982) and Bozzoli (1979, 1983, 1987). The labour history of the Witwatersrand is served as well by two successful popularising accounts: Callinicos (1980 and 1987).

The collections in which Shula Marks is one editor amount to significant re-interpretations of pre-conquest and early colonial studies of labour as well as covering the era of the mining revolution. See as well, on the commoditisation of labour and emergence of a wage-labour force: Elphick and Giliomee (1979); Worden (1985); Rayner (1981); Graves and Richardson (1980); Slater (1975); and Dubow (1982). The labour needs of the mining frontier were vast and it has been argued were central to basic transformations in state policy and the nature of imperialism in South Africa: Etherington (1979) and Marks and Trapido (1979). Apart from the Marks and Atmore and Marks and Rathbone collections, the most significant studies of how voracious demands for labour by mining capital impacted on peasant economies include Bundy (1979) (critiqued in Lewis, 1984), Beinart (1982), Crush (1984), Keegan (1986), and Trapido (1978), while the mechanisms for organising labour recruitment are the subject of Jeeves (1985).

The Boer War and the Milner reconstruction were the first important stage in which struggles over labour in an industrial era were hammered out in South Africa. Particularly relevant studies include: Richardson (1982); Denoon (1967); Ticktin (1969); Katz (1974); Levy (1982) and Johnstone (1976). Johnstone concentrates on mining in particular and on the struggles of white labour fundamental to understanding the labour segmentation that underlies white political nationalism and the apartheid system. This is also part of the importance of the work of Davies (1973 and 1979). See also Davenport (1970), Lever (1977) and Yudelman (1983). Van Onselen (1982) paints vividly the forces at play in the new urban environment. The importance of nineteenth-century Kimberley as an industrial and urban model is stressed in Turrell (1987) and Mabin (1986), while Lacey (1981) insists on the necessity of bringing analysis on to the 1930s for understanding state segregation politics. For a case study of industrial segregation in practice before World War II, see Morris and Kaplan (1976).

For an important argument on the context of rural immiseration and growing proletarianisation to political radicalisation of a qualitatively new sort, see O'Meara (1975). There is a critique shedding much light on mine labour in Moodie (1986). For other struggles of the 1940s centred around similar issues involved in working-class formation, see Hemson (1977); Stadler in Bozzoli (1979) and in Bonner (1981). Policy towards the black working class and response is highlighted in Maylam (1983) and Proctor in Bozzoli (1979).

Liberal scholarship traditionally has seen segregation and then apartheid as barriers to the effective development of labour in the South African economy; it cannot be accused of neglecting the study of labour as such. This approach is strongly pursued in Doxey (1961) and Hutt (1964). Classics of African labour and urban life include Hellman (1948) and van der Horst (1942, see also 1964) as well as the annual volumes of the South African Institute of Race Relations. By contrast, important systemic 'revisionist' critiques suggest the functionality of apartheid, particularly in the area of labour, to the specific trajectory of capital accumulation in South Africa. This is the burden of Johnstone (1970), Rex (1974), Legassick (1974a and 1974b) more circumspectly, and Wolpe (1972) more theoretically. A more complex sort of functionality sensitive to social contradictions imbues Trapido (1970–71), Bozzoli (1976) and Greenberg (1980). The most significant critique of the cheap labour theory of South African capitalism, which instead emphasises the rise of a fully proletarianised African working class distinct from the migrant stratum, lies in Hindson (1987), while Kennedy (1984) and Freund (1985) emphasise other elements in the labour force. For working-class history outside of the Witwatersrand region, see Saunders (1979); Swan (1984); Swanson (1968/69; 1976); Padayachee (1985); Hemson (1977); Phillips and van Heyningen (1981) and Nicol (1983). Unconventional liberals who reject the functionality argument and take a more sophisticated line of defence than their predecessors include Yudelman (1975) and Lipton (1985).

On accumulation and labour in agriculture, both in the contemporary period and historically, see Morris (1976), with a theoretical emphasis, and de Klerk (1984), Wilson (1972b) and Loudon (1970). Contemporary writers continue to try to come to grips with the nature of migrant labour on the countryside and on workers. Amongst the most significant are Desmond (1971), Mayer (1980) and Murray (1981) and the volumes of research produced by the Surplus People Project (1984).

The history of organised labour as resistance is prominent in Roux (1964) and Simons and Simons (1969). Other accounts that essentially represent the viewpoints of organisations or the memories of individuals but of particular value for scholarly assessment would include: Andrews (1941); Cope (1940); Sachs (1957); B. du Toit (1978) and Luckhardt and Wall (1980). With regard to black labour, one should note various assessments of the ICU in the collections listed above by such historians as Bonner and Bradford, the latter having emphasised the rural history of the ICU particularly. A more conventional political history of the ICU is to be found in Wickens (1978). For the waves of organised activity from the 1920s to the 1950s, one needs to consult these collections also as well as Welcher (1978), Feit (1975), Hirson (1977) and especially Jon Lewis (1984).

The revived non-racial trade-union movement since the early 1970s has been the subject of a vast range of occasional literature and only now are we beginning to see assessments that reflect longer-term viewpoints. Among those readings which aid an understanding of new circumstances would be Hemson (1978), D. du Toit (1981), MacShane, Plaut and Ward (1984), Friedman (1987), Berger (1982), Sitas (1984) and Morris (1986). Political interventions useful for getting a flavour of internal debates might include Foster (1982) and Plaut (1986), both from a standpoint critical of worker submersion into a nationalist political movement. Apart from the general work on politics and political economy, the writings of Eddie Webster convey some important aspects of the broader factors underlying the politics of labour at the workplace and off it over the past half-century (Webster, 1981 and 1985). A close reading of the *South African Labour Bulletin*, published for over a decade now, will be the best source of all for those who wish to pursue the subject in depth and consider the debates as they were actually happening.

FICTIONAL ACCOUNTS OF WORKING-CLASS LIFE IN AFRICA

It is hardly surprising that urban working-class life has been part of the texture of the best South African literature, which vividly advances our understanding of the themes of this book in consequence. The classic white liberal comment on urbanisation is Paton (1948) while van Bruggen was perhaps the best-known Afrikaans writer to explore creatively the migration of the 'poor whites' to the towns (1931). Peter Abrahams' *Mine Boy* (1954) is a classic socialist polemic which counters the lively and in good part admiring journalism and short stories of Nakasa, Motsisi and Themba, amongst others, who celebrated the world of crime, booze and fast women amongst the squalor of the Witwatersrand slums of the 1950s. For writing with some elements of both see La Guma (1971, 1974); the memoirs of Mphahlele (1971) and Dikobe (1983). For a powerful evocation of township revolt, see Bloom (1956) and an excellent and moving if rather apolitical tale of the life of a black working-class woman, Joubert (1980). The trade-union militancy of the past decade has inspired theatre and poetry – Sitas (ed.), *Black Mamba Rising* (1986) – while the SA Labour Bulletin has contained debates on the issue of working class culture in South Africa.

Elsewhere in Africa, a number of powerful books have considered the life of the poor, relations with other classes, the potential for revolt and the means that a working class uses to cope. Notable examples are Ngugi (1977), Mwangi (1976), Armah (1969), Iyayi (1979) and Emecheta (1979). In a class of its own both because of its desire to explain how a great strike happened, what it meant to people and its magical evocation of community life that brings to bear comparisons with such writers as Garcia Marquez, is Ousmane (1962). Ogundipe-Leslie (1981) tries to consider what a West African proletarian novel might be.

❧ BIBLIOGRAPHY ❧

Abrahams, Peter, 1954. *Mine Boy*. London, Faber.

Akpala, Agwu, 1965. 'Background of the Enugu Colliery shooting incident of 1949', *Journal of the Historical Society of Nigeria*, 3: 335–64.

Allan, William, 1965. *The African Husbandman*. Edinburgh, Oliver and Boyd.

Allen, Christopher, 1970. 'African trade unionism in microcosm: the Gambian labour movement, 1939–67', pp. 393–426, in C. Allen and R.W. Johnson (eds.), *African Perspectives*. Cambridge University Press.

Allen, V.L., 1972. 'The meaning of the working class in Africa', *Journal of Modern African Studies*, 10: 169–89.

Alpers, Edward, 1983. 'Futa Benadiir: continuity and change in the traditional cotton textile industry of Southern Somalia c.1840–1980', in Connaissance du Tiers-Monde.

Alverson, Hoyt, 1978. *Mind in the Heart of Darkness*. New Haven, Yale University Press.

Amin, Samir (ed.), 1974. *Modern Migrations in West Africa*. London, Oxford University Press.

Amsden, Alice, 1971. *International Firms and Labour in Kenya, 1945–70*. London, Cass.

Amselle, Jean-Luc, 1976. *Les Migrations africaines*. Paris, François Maspéro.

Ananaba, Wogu, 1969. *The Trade Union Movement in Nigeria*. London, C. Hurst.

1979. *The Trade Union Movement in Africa*. London, C. Hurst.

Andrews, W.H., 1941. *Class Struggles in South Africa*. Cape Town, Stewart Printing Co.

Anouma, René-Pierre, 1976. 'Une modalité du travail forcé: la prestation en Côte d'Ivoire de 1912 à la veille de la Seconde Guerre Mondiale', *Université d'Abidjan. Analles, sér. 1* (histoire), 61–86.

Armah, Ayi Kwei, 1969. *The Beautyful Ones are Not Yet Born.* New York, Heinemann.

Arrighi, Giovanni, 1970. 'International corporations, labor aristocracies and economic development in tropical Africa', in R.I. Rhodes (ed.), *Imperialism and Underdevelopment.* New York, Monthly Review Press.

   1973. 'Labour supplies in historical perspective: a study of the proletarianization of the African peasantry in Rhodesia', in Arrighi and John Saul (eds.), *Essays on the Political Economy of Africa.* New York, Monthly Review Press.

Babassana, Hilaire, 1978. *Travail forcé: expropriation et formation du salariat en Afrique noire.* Grenoble.

Balandier, Georges, 1952. 'Le développement industriel da la prolétarisation en Afrique noire', *Afrique et l'Asie*, 20: 45–53.

Bates, Robert, 1971. *Unions, Parties, and Political Development.* New Haven, Yale University Press.

Bay, Edna (ed.), 1983. *Women and Work in Africa.* Boulder, Westview Press.

Beinart, William, 1982. *The Political Economy of Pondoland.* Cambridge University Press.

Beling, W.A. (ed.), 1968. *The Role of Labor in African Nation Building.* New York, Praeger.

Berg, Elliot J., 1961. 'Backward-sloping supply functions in dual economies: the African case', *Quarterly Journal of Economics*, 75.

   1965. 'Development of a labor force in sub-Saharan Africa', *Economic Development and Cultural Change*, 13: 394–412.

   1969. 'Urban real wages and the Nigerian trade union movement', *Economic Development and Cultural Change*, 17: 604–17.

Berg, Elliot J. and Jeffrey Butler, 1964. 'Trade unions', in James Coleman and Carl Rosberg (eds.), *Political Parties and National Integration in Tropical Africa.* Berkeley, University of California Press.

Berger, Elena, 1974. *Labour, Race, and Colonial Rule.* London, Oxford University Press.

Berger, Iris, 1982. 'Sources of class consciousness: the experiences of women workers in South Africa, 1973–80', *Boston University African Studies Center Working Papers*, 55.

Bernard-Duguenet, Nicole, 1977. 'Les débuts du syndicalisme au Sénégal au temps du Front Populaire', *Le Mouvement social*, 11: 37–59.

Bernstein, Henry, 1977. 'Marxism and African history: Endre Sik and his critics', *Kenya Historical Review*, 5: 1–21.

    1977. 'Notes on capital and peasantry', *Review of African Political Economy*, 10: 60–73.

    1981. 'Notes on capital and peasantry', *Review of African Political Economy*, 21: 44–62.

Berry, Sara S., 1975. *Cocoa, Custom, and Socio-Economic Change in Rural Western Nigeria*. Oxford, Clarendon Press.

    1983. 'From peasant to artisan: motor mechanics in a Nigerian town', in Connaissance du Tiers-Monde.

Bienefeld, Manfred, 1975. 'The informal sector and peripheral capitalism', *Bulletin of the Institute of Development Studies*, 4: 53–73 (University of Sussex).

Bloom, Harry, 1956. *Episode*. London, Collins.

Bokonga, C., 1967. *Tendances fondamentales de l'évolution des relations entre travailleurs et gouvernements en Afrique*. Louvain.

Bonis, Jean, 1973. 'Syndicats et conflit collectif en Mauritanie', *Cultures et Développement*, 5: 20–50.

Bonner, Philip (ed.), 1981. *Working Papers in Southern African Studies*, 2. Johannesburg, Ravan Press.

Boserup, Ester, 1970. *Women's Role in Economic Development*. London, Allen and Unwin.

Bozzoli, Belinda, 1976. 'Managerialism and the mode of production in South Africa', *South African Labour Bulletin*, 3(8): 6–49.

    (ed.), 1979. *Labour, Townships and Protest*. Johannesburg, Ravan Press.

    1983. 'Marxism, feminism and South African studies', *Journal of Southern African Studies*, 9: 139–71.

    (ed.), 1983. *Town and Countryside in the Transvaal*. Johannesburg, Ravan Press.

    (ed.), 1987. *Class, Community and Conflict*. Johannesburg, Ravan Press.

Brabcova-Chelli, Milena, 1977. 'Guinée: action syndicale et politique avant janvier, 1956', *Archiv orientalni*, 45: 319–28 (Prague).

Brand, C.M., 1971. 'Politics and African trade unionism since federation', *Rhodesian History*, 2: 89–110.

Braundi, E.R. and A. Lettieri, 1964. 'The general strike in Nigeria', *International Socialist Journal*, 1: 598–609.

Bryceson, Deborah, 1980. 'Proletarianization of Women in Africa', *Review of African Political Economy*, 17: 4–27.

Buell, Leslie Raymond, 1928. *The Native Problem in Africa*. London, Macmillan.

Bujra, Janet, 1978–79. 'Proletarianization and the "informal economy"', *African Urban Studies*, 3: 47–66.

Bukh, Jette, 1979. *The Village Woman in Ghana*. Uppsala, Scandinavian Institute of African Studies.

Bundy, Colin, 1979. *The Rise and Fall of the South African Peasantry*. London, Heinemann.

Burawoy, Michael, 1972a. 'Another look at the mineworker', *African Social Research*, 14: 239–87.

1972b. *The Colour of Class in the Copper Mines*. Manchester University Press.

1982. 'The hidden abode of underdevelopment: labor process and the state in Zambia', *Politics and Society*, 123–66.

1985. *The Politics of Production*. London, New Left Books.

Callinicos, Luli, 1980. *Gold and Workers, 1886–1924: People's History of South Africa*, 1. Johannesburg, Ravan Press.

1987. *Working*. Johannesburg, Ravan Press.

Canadian Journal of African Studies, 1985. Special Issue on Modes of Production in Africa.

Chaulet, Claudine, 1971. *La Mitidja autogerée*. Algiers, SNED.

Chauncey, George, Jr, 1981. 'The locus of reproduction: women's labour in the Zambian copperbelt, 1927–53', *Journal of Southern African Studies*, 7: 135–64.

Chavanduka, George, 1972. 'Farm labourers in Rhodesia', *Rhodesian Journal of Economics*, 6: 18–25.

Chege, Michael, 1981. 'A tale of two slums: electoral politics in Mathare and Dagoretti', *ROAPE*, 20.

Chrétien, J.P., 1978. 'Des sedentaires devenu migrants: motifs des départs des burundais et des rwandais vers l'Uganda', *Cultures et Développement*, 10: 71–102.

Clarence-Smith, W.G., 1979a. 'Slaves, commoners and landlords in Bulozi', *Journal of African History*, 20: 219–34.

1979b. *Slaves, Peasants and Capitalists in Southern Angola, 1840–*

1926. Cambridge University Press.

Clarke, Duncan, 1974a. *Contract Workers and Underdevelopment in Rhodesia*, Gwelo, Mambo Press.

1974b. *Domestic Workers in Rhodesia*. Gwelo, Mambo Press.

1977a. *Agricultural and Plantation Workers in Rhodesia*. Gwelo, Mambo Press.

1977b. *Unemployment and Economic Structure in Rhodesia*. Gwelo, Mambo Press.

Clayton, Anthony and D.C. Savage, 1974. *Government and Labour in Kenya, 1895–1963*. London, Cass.

Cleave, John, 1974. *African Farmers: Labor Use in the Development of Smallholder Agriculture*. New York, Praeger.

Cock, Jacklyn, 1980. *Maids and Madams*. Johannesburg, Ravan Press.

Cock, Jacklyn and E. Emdon, 1987. 'Let me make history please: the story of Johanna Masilela, childminder', in Bozzoli (1987).

Cohen, Robin, 1971. 'Further comment on the Kilby/Weeks debate', *Journal of Developing Areas*, 5: 155–64.

1974. *Labour and Politics in Nigeria*. London, Heinemann.

1976. 'From peasants to workers', in P. Gutkind and I. Wallerstein (eds.), *The Political Economy of Africa*. Beverly Hills, Sage.

1980. 'Resistance and hidden forms of consciousness among African workers', *Review of African Political Economy*, 19: 8–22.

Cohen, Robin and D. Michael, 1976. 'The revolutionary potential of the African lumpenproletariat: a skeptical view', *Bulletin of the Institute of Development Studies*, 5: 31–42 (University of Sussex).

Connaissance du Tiers-Monde, Laboratoire. Université de Paris 7, 1983. *Enterprises et entrepreneurs en Afrique XIXe et XXe siècles*. Paris, L'Harmattan.

Conti, Anna, 1979. 'Capitalist organisation of production through non-capitalist relations: women's role in a pilot resettlement in Upper Volta', *Review of African Political Economy*, 15/16: 75–92.

Conway, H.E., 1968. 'Labour protest activity in Sierra Leone', *Labour History*, 15: 49–63 (Canberra).

Cooper, Frederick, 1977. *Plantation Slavery on the East Coast of Africa*. New Haven, Yale University Press.

1979. 'The problem of slavery in African studies', *Journal of African History*, 20: 103–25.

1981a. *From Slaves to Squatters*. New Haven, Yale University Press.

1981b. 'Peasants, capitalists and historians', *Journal of Southern African Studies*, 7: 284–314.

(ed.), 1984. *The Struggle for the City*. London/Beverly Hills, Sage.

1987. *On the African Waterfront*. New Haven, Yale University Press.

Copans, Jean, 1981. 'Les classes ouvrières d'Afrique noire: bibliographie selectionnée, classée, commentée', *Cahiers d'études africaines*, 22: 405–29.

Cope, R.K., 1940. *Comrade Bill*. Cape Town, Stewart Printing Co.

Coquery-Vidrovitch, Catherine, 1971. 'De la traite des esclaves à l'exportation de l'huile de palme et des palmistes au Dahomey, XIXe siècle', in Claude Meillassoux (ed.), *Development of Indigenous Trade and Markets in West Africa*. London, Oxford University Press.

1976. 'Research on an African mode of production', in Gutkind and Waterman (eds.), *African Social Studies: A Radical Reader*. London, Heinemann.

Cowan, E.A., 1961. *The Evolution of Trade Unionism in Ghana*. Accra, Ghana TUC.

Crisp, Jeff, 1978. 'The labouring poor, trade unions and political change in Ghana', *Manpower and Unemployment Research*, 11: 93–100.

1979. 'Union atrophy and worker revolt: labour protest at Tarkwa goldfields, Ghana, 1968–69', *Canadian Journal of African Studies* 13: 265–94.

1984. 'Productivity and protest: scientific management in the Ghanaian gold mines, 1947–56', in Cooper, ed. (1984).

Cruise O'Brien, Rita (ed.), 1979. *The Political Economy of Development: Dependence in Senegal*. Beverly Hills, Sage.

Crush, Jonathan, 1984. 'Uneven labour migration in southern Africa: conceptions and misconceptions', *South African Geographical Journal*, 66: 115–31.

Damachi, Ukandi, 1974. *The Role of Trade Unions in the Development Process with a Case Study of Ghana*. New York, Praeger.

Damachi, Ukandi et al., 1979. *Industrial Relations in Africa*. London, Macmillan.

Davenport, T.R.H., 1970. 'The triumph of Colonel Stallard', *South African Historical Journal*, 2: 77–96.

David, Philippe, 1980. *Les Navétanes*. Dakar/Abidjan, Nouvelles Editions Africaines.

Davies, Ioan, 1966. *African Trade Unions*. Harmondsworth, Penguin.

Davies, Robert, 1973. 'The white working class in South Africa', *New Left Review*, 82: 40–59.

   1979. *Capital, State and White Labour in South Africa, 1900–60*. Brighton, Harvester.

de Jonge, Klaas, 1979. 'Peasant fishermen and capitalist development in Senegal', *ROAPE*, 15/16: 105–23.

de Klerk, Michael, 1984. 'Seasons that will never return', *Journal of Southern African Studies*, 11(1): 84–105.

de Kiewiet, C.W., 1941. *A History of South Africa: Social and Economic*. London, Oxford University Press.

de Miras, Claude, 1984. 'De la formation du capital privé à l'économie populaire spontanée', *Politique Africaine*, 14: 92–109.

Demunter, Paul, 1972. 'Structure de classes et luttes de classes dans le Congo colonial', *Contradictions*, 1: 67–109 (Brussels).

Denoon, D.J.N., 1967. 'The Transvaal Labour Crisis, 1901–06', *Journal of African History*, 8: 481–94.

Derman, William, 1972. *Serfs, Peasants and Socialists*. Berkeley, University of California Press.

Desmond, Cosmas, 1971. *The Discarded People*. Harmondsworth, Penguin.

Dikobe, Modikwe, 1983. *The Dispossessed*. Johannesburg, Ravan.

Diop, Abdoulaye-Bara, 1965. *Société toucouleur et migration*. Dakar, Université de Dakar.

   1981. *La société wolof*. Paris, Karthala.

Diouf, Made B., 1983. 'Migration artisanale et solidarité villageoise: le cas de Kanèn Njob au Sénégal', in Connaissance du Tiers-Monde.

Doucy, A., 1954. 'Le rôle des influences coutumières sur les travailleurs du Congo', *Revue de l'Institut de Sociologie Solvay*, 27.

Doucy, A. and Feldheim, P., 1952. *Problèmes du travail et politique sociale au Congo belge*. Brussels, Librairie Encyclopédique.

Doxey, G.V., 1961. *The Industrial Colour Bar in South Africa*. Cape Town, Oxford University Press.

Drake, St. Clair and Lacey, L.A., 1966. 'Government Versus the Unions: The Sekondi-Takoradi Strike of 1961', in Gwendolen Carter (ed.), *Politics in Africa: Seven Cases*. New York, Harcourt, Brace.

Dubow, Saul, 1982. *Land, Labour and Merchant Capital: The Experience of the Graaff Reinet District in the Pre-Industrial Rural Economy of the Cape, 1852–72*. University of Cape Town Centre for

African Studies Communications, 6.

Duffy, James, 1967. *A Question of Slavery*. London, Oxford University Press.

Dumett, Raymond, 1979. 'Precolonial mining and the state in the Akan region', in George Dalton (ed.), *Research in Economic Anthropology*, 2: 37–68.

du Toit, Bettie, 1978. *Ukubamba Amadolo: Workers' Struggles in the South African Textile Industry*. London, Onyx Press.

Du Toit, Darcy, 1981. *Capital and Labour in South Africa: Class Struggles in the 1970s*. London, Kegan Paul International.

Elkan, Walter, 1960. *Migrants and Proletarians*. London, Oxford University Press.

  1976. 'Is a proletariat emerging in Nairobi?', *Economic Development and Cultural Change*, 14: 695–706.

  1980. 'Labour migration from Botswana, Lesotho and Swaziland', *Economic Development and Cultural Change*, 28: 583–96.

Elphick, Richard and Hermann Giliomee (eds.), 1979. *The Shaping of South African Society 1652–1820*. Cape Town, Longman Penguin.

Emecheta, Buchi, 1979. *The Joys of Motherhood*. New York, George Braziller.

Epstein, A.L., 1958. *Politics in an Urban African Community*. Manchester University Press.

Etherington, Norman, 1979. 'Labour supply and the genesis of South African confederation in the 1870s', *Journal of African History*, 20: 134–52.

Fall, Babacar, 1976/77. 'Le travail forcé au Sénégal'. Unpublished master's thesis, University of Dakar.

  1983. 'Les enterprises agricoles privées au Soudan Français: le cas de la Société Anonyme des Cultures de Diakandape', in Connaissance du Tiers-Monde.

Fanon, Frantz, 1963. *The Wretched of the Earth*. New York, Grove Press.

Fapohunda, Olanrewaju and Harold Lubell, 1978. *Lagos: Urban Development and Employment*. Geneva, ILO

Fawzi, S., 1957. *The Labour Movement in the Sudan*. London, Oxford University Press.

Feit, Edward, 1975. *Workers Without Unions*. Hamden, Conn., Archon Books.

Fetter, Bruce, 1973. 'L'Union Minière du Haut-Katanga 1920–40: la naissance d'une sous-culture totalitaire', *Cahiers du CEDAF*, 6.

1976. *The Creation of Elisabethville, 1910–40*. Stanford, Hoover Institution Press.

Fetter, Bruce and Marvin Miracle, 1970. 'Backward sloping supply functions and African economic development', *Economic Development and Cultural Change*, 18: 240–51.

Foster, Joe, 1982. 'The workers' struggle: where does FOSATU stand?', *Review of African Political Economy*, 24: 95–113.

Fraenkel, Meran, 1964. *Tribe and Class in Monrovia*. London, Oxford University Press.

Fransman, Martin (ed.), 1982. *Industry and Accumulation in Africa*, London, Hutchinson.

Freund, Bill, 1981a. *Capital and Labour in the Nigerian Tin Mines*. Harlow, Longmans.

1981b. 'Labour migration to the Northern Nigerian tin mines, 1903–45', *Journal of African History*, 22: 73–84.

1982. 'Theft and social protest among the tin miners of Northern Nigeria', *Radical History Review*, 26: 66–88.

1985. 'The social character of industry in South Africa 1915–45', *African Studies Institute*, Johannesburg, seminar paper.

Freund, Bill and Bob Shenton, 1977. 'Vent-for-surplus theory and the economic history of West Africa', *Savanna*, 6: 191–96.

Friedland, William, 1967. 'Co-operation, conflict and conscription: TANU-TFL relations, 1956–64', in Jeffrey Butler and A.A. Castagno (eds.), *Boston Papers in African Studies*. New York.

1969. *Vuta Kamba: The Development of Trade Unions in Tanganyika*. Stanford, Hoover Institution Press.

1974. 'African trade union studies: analysis of two decades', *Cahiers d'études africaines*, 14: 575–89.

Friedman, Steven, 1987. *Building Tomorrow Today*. Johannesburg, Ravan.

Furedi, Frank, 1973. 'The African crowd in Nairobi', *Journal of African History*, 14: 75–90.

1976. 'The Kikuyu squatters in the Rift Valley', in B. Ogot (ed.), *Hadith*, 5: 177–94.

Gaitskell, Deborah et al., 1984. 'Class, race and gender: domestic workers in South Africa', *ROAPE*, 27/28.

Geiss, Immanuel, 1965. *Gewerkschaften in Afrika*. Hannover, Verlag für

Literatur und Zeitgeschehen.

Gerritsen, Rolf, 1972. 'Evolution of the Ghana TUC under the CPP: towards a re-interpretation', *Transactions of the Historical Society of Ghana*, 13: 229–44.

Glass, Yetta, 1960. *The Black Industrial Worker*. Johannesburg, National Institute for Personnel Research.

Goldberg, Melvin, 1981. 'Formulating Worker Consciousness', *Social Dynamics*, 7: 32–41. Cape Town.

Goody, Jack, 1971. *Technology, Tradition and the State in Africa*. London, Oxford University Press.

Gordon, Robert, 1977. *Mines, Masters and Migrants*. Johannesburg, Ravan Press.

Graves, Adrian and Peter Richardson, 1980. 'Plantations in the political economy of colonial sugar production: Natal and Queensland, 1860–1914', *Journal of Southern African Studies*, 6: 214–29.

Gray, Paul, 1981. *Unions and Leaders in Ghana*. Owerri/New York, Conch Magazine.

Greenberg, Stanley, 1980. *Race and State in Capitalist Development*. New Haven, Yale University Press.

Grillo, Ralph, 1973. *African Railwaymen*. Cambridge University Press.
   1974. *Race, Class and Militancy: An African Trade Union, 1939–65*. New York, Chandler.

Guérin, Daniel, 1964. 'Au Ghana, syndicalisme et socialisme', *Présence Africaine*, 23: 16–25.

Gugler, J. 'The impact of labour migration on society and economy in sub-Saharan Africa', *African Social Research*, 6: 465–86.

Gulliver, P.H., 1955. *Labour Migration in a Rural Economy*. Kampala, East African Institute of Social Research.

Gutkind, Peter, 1974. 'The emerging African urban proletariat', McGill University Centre for Developing Area Studies Occasional Papers, 8.
   1975. 'The view from below: political consciousness of the urban poor in Ibadan', *Cahiers d'études africaines*, 15: 5–35.

Gutkind, Peter, Robin Cohen and Jean Copans (eds.), 1979. *African Labor History*. Beverly Hills/London, Sage.

Guy, Jeff, 1979. *The Destruction of the Zulu Kingdom*. London, Longmans.

Guyer, Jane, 1980a. *Household Budgets and Women's Incomes*. Boston

University African Studies Center Working Papers, 28.

1980b. 'Food, cocoa and the division of labour by sex in two West African societies', *Comparative Studies in Society and History*, 22.

1982. 'Cultivation systems and the timing of work'. Paper presented at Kinship and Capitalism Conference, Cambridge, Mass.

Hansen, K.T., 1980. 'The urban informal sector as a development issue', *Urban Anthropologist*, 9: 2.

1986. 'Domestic service in Zambia', *Journal of Southern African Studies*, 13(1): 57–81.

Harries-Jones, Peter, 1975. *Freedom and Labour*. Oxford, Blackwell.

Harris, Marvin, 1959. 'Labour emigration among the Mozambique Thonga: cultural and political factors', *Africa*, 29: 50–65, with a 'Comment' by A. Rita Ferreira, 1960. *Africa*, 30.

Harris, Peter, 1975. 'Industrial workers in Rhodesia, 1946–72', *Journal of Southern African Studies*, 1: 139–61.

Hart, Keith, 1973. 'Informal income opportunities and urban employment in Ghana', *Journal of Modern African Studies*, 11: 141–69.

1976. 'The politics of unemployment in Ghana', *African Affairs*, 75: 488–97.

Hauser, André, 1968. *Les ouvriers de Dakar: étude psychosociologique*. Paris, ORSTOM.

Hay, Margaret, 1976. 'Luo women and economic change during the colonial period', in Nancy Hafkin and Edna Bay (eds.), *Women in Africa*. Stanford University Press.

Hellman, Ellen, 1948. *Rooiyard*. Rhodes-Livingstone Papers 13 and Cape Town, Oxford University Press.

Hemson, David, 1977. 'Dock workers, labour circulation and class struggles in Durban, 1945–59', *Journal of Southern African Studies*, 4: 88–124.

1978. 'Trade unionism and the struggle for liberation in South Africa', *Capital and Class*, 6: 1–41.

1979. 'Are migrant workers a sub-proletariat? The dockworkers of Durban'. University of Dar es Salaam Department of History seminar paper.

Henderson, Ian, 1973a. 'Early African leadership: the copperbelt disturbances of 1935 and 1940', *Journal of Southern African Studies*, 2: 83–97.

1973b. 'Wage earners and political protest in colonial Africa', *African*

Affairs, 57: 288–99.

1974. 'The limits of colonial power: race and labour problems in colonial Zambia, 1900–53', *Journal of Imperial and Commonwealth Studies*, 2: 297–307.

Henn, Jeanne, 1982. 'Production theory and the study of rural women's work: cases from Cameroon and Tanzania'. Paper presented at Kinship and Capitalist Conference, Cambridge, Mass.

Hill, Polly, 1963. *The Migrant Cocoa Farmers of Southern Ghana*. Cambridge University Press.

Hinchliffe, Keith, 1973. 'The Kaduna textile workers: characteristics of an African industrial labour force', *Savanna*, 2: 27–37.

1974. 'Labour aristocracy: a Northern Nigeria case study', *Journal of Modern African Studies*, 12: 57–67.

Hindson, Doug., 1987. *Pass Controls and the Urban African Proletariat*. Johannesburg, Ravan.

Hirson, Baruch, 1977. 'Reorganisation of African trade unions in Johannesburg, 1936–42'. Institute of Commonwealth Studies (London). Collected Seminar Papers on the Societies of Southern Africa in the Nineteenth and Twentieth Centuries, 7.

Hodgkin, Thomas, 1956. *Nationalism in Colonial Africa*, London, Frederick Muller.

Hogendorn, J.S., 1976. 'The vent-for-surplus model and African cash agriculture to 1914', *Savanna*, 5: 15–28.

Hopkins, A.G. 1966. 'The Lagos strike of 1897', *Past and Present*, 35: 135–55.

1973. *Economic History of West Africa*. London, Longmans.

Hugon, Philippe, 1983. 'Le développement des petites entreprises à Antananarivo: l'exemple d'un processus involuntif', in Connaissance du Tiers-Monde.

Hutt, W.H., 1964. *The Economics of the Colour Bar*. London, Deutsch.

Hyden, Goran, 1980. *Beyond Ujamaa in Tanzania*. London, Heinemann.

Iliffe, John, 1980. 'Wage labour and urbanisation', in M.H. Kaniki (ed.), *Tanzania under Colonial Rule*. Harlow, Longmans.

Ivanov, Y.M., 1979. *Agrarian Reforms and Hired Labor in Africa*. Moscow, Progress Publishers.

Iyayi, Felix, 1979. *Violence*. London, Longmans.

Jackson, Dudley, 1979. 'The disappearance of strikes in Tanzania, incomes policy and industrial democracy', *Journal of Modern African*

Studies, 17: 219–51.

Jackson, Sam, 1978. 'Hausa women on strike', *Review of African Political Economy*, 13: 21–36.

Jaggar, P.J., 1973. 'Kano city blacksmiths: precolonial distribution, structure and organisation', *Savanna*, 2: 11–25.

Janmohamed, Karim, 1976. 'African labourers in Mombasa c.1895–1940', in B. Ogot (ed.), *Hadith*, 5: 154–76.

Jeeves, Alan, 1975. 'The control of migratory labour in the South African gold mines in the era of Kruger and Milner', *Journal of Southern African Studies*, 2: 3–29.
    1985. *Migrant Labour in South Africa's Mining Economy*. McGill-Queen's University Press, Montreal.

Jeffries, Richard, 1975. 'The labour aristocracy? a Ghana case study', *Review of African Political Economy*, 3: 59–70.
    1978. *Class, Ideology and Power in Africa: The Railwaymen of Sekondi*. Cambridge University Press.

Jewsiewicki, Bogumil, Kiloma Lema and Jean-Luc Vellut, 1973. 'Documents pour servir à l'histoire sociale du Zaïre: grèves dans le Bas-Congo (Bas-Zaïre) en 1945', *Etudes d'histoire africaine*, 5: 155–88.

Johns, Sheridan, 1967. 'The birth of non-white trade unionism in South Africa', *Race*, 9: 173–92.

Johnstone, Frederick, 1970. 'White supremacy and white prosperity in South Africa today', *African Affairs*, 69: 124–40.
    1976. *Class, Race and Gold*. London, Routledge Kegan Paul.

Joseph, Richard, 1974. 'Settlers, strikers, and sans-travail: the Douala riots of September 1945', *Journal of African History*, 15: 669–87.

Joubert, Elsa, 1980. *Poppie*. London, Coronet Books.

Kadalie, Clements, 1970. *My Life and the ICU*. London, Cass.

Kane, Francine, 1977. 'Femmes proletaires du Sénégal, à la ville et aux champs', *Cahiers d'études africaines*, 17: 77–94.

Kapferer, Bruce, 1972. *Strategy and Transaction in an African Factory*. Manchester University Press.
    1976. 'Conflict and process in a Zambian mine community', *Political Anthropology*, 1: 50–79.

Katz, Elaine, 1974. 'White workers' grievances and the industrial colour bar', *South African Journal of Economics*, 42: 127–56.

Kea, Ray, 1983. *Settlement, Trade and Politics in the Seventeenth Century Gold Coast*. Baltimore, Johns Hopkins University Press.

Keegan, Timothy, 1986. *Rural Transformation in an Industrialising South Africa*. Harlow, Longmans.

Kennedy, Brian, 1984. *A Tale of Two Mining Cities*. Ad Donker, Johannesburg and Melbourne University Press.

Kilby, Peter, 1967. 'Industrial relations and wage determination', *Journal of Developing Areas*, 1: 490–520 and reply (1968) in *Journal of Developing Areas*, 3: 19–26.

King, Kenneth, 1977. *The African Artisan: Education and the Informal Sector in Kenya*. London, Heinemann.

Kitching, Gavin, 1980. *Class and Economic Change in Kenya*. New Haven, Yale University Press.

Kjekshus, Helge, 1977. *Labour in Tanzania*, introducer. University of Dar es Salaam Studies in Political Science 5.

Kraus, Jon, 1979. 'Strikes and labour power in Ghana', *Development and Change*, 10: 159–86.

Kriszan, L., 1970. *Aspects of an Analysis of the Labor Structure of the Nigerian Working Class*. Budapest, Hungarian Academy of Sciences, Centre for Afro-Asian Research.

Lacey, Marion, 1981. *Working for Boroko: Origins of a Coercive Labour System in South Africa*. Johannesburg, Ravan Press.

La Guma, Alex (ed.), 1971. *Apartheid: A Collection of Writings on South African Racism by South Africans*. New York, International Publishers.

1974. *The Stone Country*. London, Heinemann.

Lakroum, Monique, 1983. *Le travail inégal: paysans et salariés sénégalais face à la crise des années trente*. Paris, L'Harmattan.

LeBrun, Olivier and Chris Gerry, 1975. 'Petty producers and capitalism', *Review of African Political Economy*, 3: 20–32.

Legassick, Martin, 1974a. 'Legislation, ideology and economy in post-1974 South Africa', *Journal of Southern African Studies*, 1: 5–34.

1974b. 'South Africa: capital accumulation and violence', *Economy and Society*, 3.

1975. 'The records of British firms in South Africa in the context of the political economy', *South African Labour Bulletin*, 2/1: 7–36.

Leger, Jean, 1985. *Towards Safer Underground Gold Mining*. Johannesburg, University of the Witwatersrand Sociology Department.

Leitner, Kerstin, 1972. *Workers, Trade Unions and Peripheral Capitalism in Kenya after Independence*. Frankfurt am Main.

1976. 'The situation of agricultural workers in Kenya', *Review of African Political Economy*, 6: 34–50.

Lever, Jeff, 1977. 'Capital and labour in South Africa: the passage of the Industrial Conciliation Act 1924', *South African Labour Bulletin*, 3/10: 4–31.

Levy, Norman, 1982. *Foundations of the South African Cheap Labour System*. London, Routledge & Kegan Paul.

Lewis, Jack, 1984. 'The rise and fall of the South African peasantry: a critique and reassessment'. *Journal of Southern African Studies*, 11(1): 1–24.

Lewis, Jon, 1984. *Industrialisation and Trade Union Organisation in South Africa 1924–55*. Cambridge University Press.

Lewis, W. Arthur, 1954. 'Economic development with unlimited supplies of labour', *Manchester School of Economic and Social Studies*, 22: 139–91.

Lipton, Merle, 1986. *Capitalism and Apartheid*. Cape Town, David Philip.

Lonsdale, John and Bruce Berman, 1979. 'Coping with the contradictions: the development of the colonial state in Kenya', *Journal of African History*, 10: 487–506.

1980. 'Crises of accumulation, coercion and the colonial state: development of the labour control system in Kenya, 1919–29', *Canadian Journal of African Studies*, 14: 55–82.

Loudon, J.B., 1970. *White Farmers and Black Labour-Tenants*. Cambridge/Leiden, Afrika Studie Centrum.

Lovejoy, Paul, 1979. 'Characteristics of plantations in the nineteenth century Sokoto Caliphate', *American Historical Review*, 84: 1267–92.

(ed.), 1981. *The Ideology of Slavery in Africa*. Beverly Hills/London, Sage.

1983. *Transformations in Slavery*. Cambridge University Press.

Low, D.A. and John Lonsdale, 1976. 'Introduction: towards the new order, 1945–63', in Alison Smith and D.A. Low, *History of East Africa III*. Oxford, Clarendon Press.

Lubeck, Paul, 1978. 'Labour in Kano since the petroleum boom', *Review of African Political Economy*, 13: 37–46.

1979. 'The value of multiple methods in researching third world strikes: a Nigerian example', *Development and Change*, 10: 301–19.

Luckhardt, Ken and Brenda Wall, 1980. *Organize . . . or Starve: The History of the South African Congress of Trade Unions*. London, Lawrence and Wishart.

Lugard, Lord, 1929. *The Dual Mandate in British Tropical Africa*. London, Wm. Blackwood and Sons.

Lux, André, 1962. *Le marché du travail en Afrique noire*. Louvain, Institut de recherches économiques sociales et politiques.

Mabin, Alan, 1986. 'Labour, Capital, Class Struggle and the Origins of Residential Segregation in Kimberley 1880–1920', *Journal of Historical Geography*, 12(1): 4–26.

Mackenzie, J.M., 1970. 'African labour in the chartered company period', *Rhodesian History*, 1: 43–58.

Macmillan, W.M., 1938. *Africa Emergent*. London, Faber and Faber.

Macshane, D., Plaut and Ward, 1984. *Power!* Nottingham, Spokesman.

Magubane, Bernard, 1971. 'A critical look at indices used in the study of social change in colonial Africa', *Current Anthropology*, 12: 419–46.

Malaba, Luke, 1980. 'Supply, control and organisation of African labour in Rhodesia', *Review of African Political Economy*, 18: 7–28.

Mapolu, Henry (ed.), 1976. *Workers and Management*. Dar es Salaam, Tanzania Publishing House.

Marks, Shula and Stanley Trapido, 1979. 'Lord Milner and the South African war', *History Workshop Journal*, 8: 50–80.

Marks, Shula and Antony Atmore (eds.), 1980. *Economy and Society in Pre-industrial South Africa*. Harlow, Longmans.

Marks, Shula and Richard Rathbone (eds.), 1982. *Industrialization and Social Change in South Africa*. Harlow, Longmans.

Martens, George (ed.), 1977. *African Trade Unionism*. Boston, G.K. Hall.

Massey, David, 1980. 'The changing economy of migrant labour in Botswana', *South African Labour Bulletin*, 5/5: 4–26.

Marx, Karl and Friedrich Engels, 1961. *The Communist Manifesto* in *Essential Works of Marxism*. New York, Bantam Books.

Mayer, Philip (ed.). *Black Villagers in an Industrial Society*. Cape Town, Oxford University Press.

Maylam, Paul, 1983. 'The Black Belt: African Squatters in Durban 1935–50', *Canadian Journal of African Studies*, 17: 413–28.

Mayson, Dew Tuan-Wleh and Amos Sawyer, 1979. 'Labour in Liberia',

Review of African Political Economy, 14: 3–15.

McNamara, J.K., 1978. 'Migration routes to the gold mines and compound accommodation, 1889–1912', *South African Labour Bulletin*, 4/3: 7–28.

Meillassoux, Claude, 1972. 'From reproduction to production', *Economy and Society*, 1: 93–105.

    (ed.), 1975. *L'esclavage en Afrique précoloniale*. Paris, François Maspero.

    1981. *Maidens, Meal and Money*. Cambridge University Press.

Melson, Robert, 1970. 'Nigerian politics and the general strike of 1964', in Robert Rotberg and Ali Mazrui (eds.), *Protest and Power in Black Africa*. New York, Oxford University Press.

    1973. 'The political dilemmas of Nigerian labor', in Ukandi Damachi and Hans-Dieter Seibel (eds.), *Social Change and Economic Development in Nigeria*. New York, Praeger.

Mendes, Afonso, 1958. *A Huila é Moçâmedes*. Lisbon, Junta de Investigações do Ultramar Centro de Estudos Politicas e Soçais.

Meynaud, Jean and Anisse Salah-Bey, 1962. *Fondements idéologiques du mouvement syndical africain*. Paris, Centre d'études des relations internationales.

    1967. *Trade Unionism in Africa*. London, Methuen.

Mihyo, Paschal, 1975. 'The struggle for workers' control in Tanzania', *Review of African Political Economy*, 4: 62–85.

Mitchell, J. Clyde, 1956. *The Kalela Dance*. Rhodes-Livingstone Paper 27.

    1961a. 'The causes of labour migration' in *Commission for Technical Co-operation in Africa South of the Sahara*. Abidjan. Sixth Inter-African Labour Conference Publication 79.

    1961b. 'Wages, Labour and African Population Movements in Central Africa', in K. Barbour and R.M. Prothero (eds.), *Essays on African Population*. New York, Praeger.

    1969. 'Structural Plurality, Urbanization and Labour Circulation in Southern Rhodesia', in J.A. Jackson (ed.), *Migration*. Cambridge University Press.

Miti, Katabaro, 1985. 'Politique Nguu Kazi à Dar es Salaam', *Politique Africaine*, 17: 83–104.

Moodie, Dunbar, 1983. 'Mine culture and miners' identity on the South African gold mines' in Bozzoli.

1986. 'The moral economy of the black miners' strike of 1946', *Journal of Southern African Studies*, 13(1): 1–35.

Moorsom, Richard, 1977. 'Underdevelopment, contract labour and worker consciousness in Namibia, 1915–72', *Journal of Southern African Studies*, 4: 52–87.

1979. 'Labour consciousness and the 1971–72 contract workers' strike in Namibia', *Development and Change*, 10: 205–31.

Morice, Alain, 1982. 'Underpaid child labour and social reproduction: apprenticeship in Kaolack, Sénégal', *Development and Change*, 13: 515–26.

Morris, Mike, 1976. 'The development of capitalism in South African agriculture: class struggle in the countryside', *Economy and Society*, 5: 292–343.

1986. 'Stevedoring and the general workers union', *South African Labour Bulletin*, 11(3): 90–114; (5): 100–18.

Morris, Mike and Dave Kaplan, 1976. 'Labour policy in a state corporation: a case study of the South African iron and steel industry', *South African Labour Bulletin*, 2/6–7.

Moyo, E., 1973. 'Shabani and the outbreak of violence' in S.E. Wilmer (ed.) *Zimbabwe Now*. London, Rex Collings.

Mphahlele, Ezekiel, 1971. *Down Second Avenue*. London, Faber and Faber.

Mukenge, Evariste, 1971. 'L'évolution politique du mouvement syndical congolais', *Problèmes sociaux zaïrois*, 94/95: 3–55.

Mulot, Francis, 1979. 'Syndicalisme et politique au Sénégal, 1968–76', *Revue française d'études politiques africaines*, 158: 53–90.

Murray, Colin, 1981. *Families Divided*. Cambridge University Press.

Murteira, Mario, 1960. *Sindicalismo e Evolução Social no Africa ão sul do Sahara*. Lisbon, Junta de Investigações do Ultramar, Centro de Estudos Politicos e Soçiais.

Mwangi, Meja, 1976. *Going Down River Road*. London, Heinemann.

Myint, Hla, 1965. *The Economies of the Developing Countries*. London, Hutchinson.

Nattrass, Jill, 1981. *The South African Economy; Its Growth and Change*. Cape Town, Oxford University Press.

Naville, Pierre (ed.), 1952. 'Le travail en Afrique noire', *Présence Africaine*.

Ndiaye, Massata Abdou, 1964. *Le mouvement syndical africain*.

Conakry, Imp. Patrice Lumumba.

Ndour, Biram, 1981. 'Le mouvement ouvrier sénégalais à ses débuts', *Jonction*, 5: 21–30.

Nelson, Nici (ed.), 1981. *African Women in the Development Process*. London, Cass.

Newbury, Colin, 1975. 'Historical aspects of manpower and migration, in Africa south of the Sahara' in L. Gann and P. Duignan (eds.), *Colonialism in Africa*, 4. Cambridge University Press.

Ngugi wa Thiongo, 1977. *Petals of Blood*. London, Heinemann.

Nguyen Van Chi-Bonnardel, Régine, 1983. 'Quel avenir pour les artisans sénégalais?', in Connaissance du Tiers-Monde.

Nicol, Martin, 1983. 'Riches from rags: bosses and unions in the Cape clothing industry 1926–37', *Journal of Southern African Studies*, 9(2): 239–57.

Ninine, Jules, 1932. *Le main d'oeuvre indigène dans les colonies: thèse de doctorat*. Paris.

November, A., 1965. *L'évolution du mouvement syndical en Afrique occidentale*. The Hague/Paris, Mouton.

Nyerere, Julius, 1968. *Freedom and Socialism*. London, Oxford University Press.

Nzula, Albert, I. Potekhin and Aleksander Zusmanovich, 1979. *Forced Labour in Africa*. London, Zed Press.

Obbo, Christine, 1980. *African Women: Their Struggle for Economic Independence*. London, Zed Press.

O'Brien, Jay, 1983. 'The formation of the agricultural labour force in Sudan', *ROAPE* 26, 15–34.

Ogundipe-Leslie, Omolara, 1981. 'The first Nigerian "proletarian novel"?', *Review of African Political Economy*, 22: 108–15.

Ohadike, P.O., 1969. 'Development of and factors in the employment of migrants in the copper mines of Zambia, 1940–66', *Zambian Papers*, 4.

Olivier, Lord, 1929. *White Capital and Coloured Labour*. London, Hogarth Press.

O'Meara, Dan, 1975. 'The 1946 African miners' strike and the political economy of South Africa', *Journal of Commonwealth and Comparative Politics*, 12: 146–73.

Oppong, Christine (ed.), 1983. *Female and Male in West Africa*. London, Allen and Unwin.

Orde Brown, G. St. J., 1932. *The African Labourer*. London, Oxford University Press.

Orimalade, Olucronke, 1974. *Bibliography on Labour in Nigeria*. Lagos, National Library of Nigeria.

Osoba, Segun, 1969. 'The phenomenon of labour migration in the era of British colonial rule', *Journal of the Historical Society of Nigeria*, 4: 515–38.

Ousmane, Sembène, 1962. *God's Bits of Wood*. New York, Heinemann.

Oyemakinde, W., 1974a. 'The Nigerian general strike of 1964', *Genève-Afrique*, 13: 53–71.

    1974b. 'Railway construction and operations in Nigeria, 1895–1911', *Journal of the Historical Society of Nigeria*, 7: 303–24.

Padayachee, Vishnu et al. 1985. *Indian Workers and Trade Unions in Durban, 1930–50*. Institute for Social and Economic Research Report 20, University of Durban-Westville.

Padmore, George, 1936. *How Britain Rules Africa*. London, Wishart.

Palmer, Robin and Neil Parsons (eds.), 1977. *The Roots of Rural Poverty in Central and Southern Africa*. London, Heinemann.

Parkin, David, 1976. 'Migration, settlement and the politics of unemployment', in D. Parkin (ed.), *Town and Country in Central and East Africa*. London, Oxford University Press.

Parpart, Jane, 1982a. 'Class consciousness among Zambian copper miners, 1950–66'. Boston University African Studies Center Working Papers 53.

    1982b. 'The "labor aristocracy" thesis considered once again: the Northern Rhodesian copperbelt, 1926–66'. Boston University African Studies Center Working Papers 56.

    1983. *Capital and Labor on the African Copperbelt*. Philadelphia, Temple University Press.

Parson, Jack, 1980. 'The working class, the state and social change in Botswana', *South African Labour Bulletin*, 5/5: 45–55.

Paton, Alan, 1948. *Cry, the Beloved Country*. London, Cape.

Peace, Adrian, 1979. *Choice, Class and Conflict: A Study of Southern Nigerian Factory Workers*. London, Harvester Press.

Peil, Margaret, 1970. *The Ghanaian Factory Worker*. Cambridge University Press.

Penvenne, Jeanne, 1979a. 'Attitudes towards race and work in Mozambique: Lourenço Marques, 1900–74'. Boston University African

Studies Center Working Papers 16.

1979b. 'Forced labor and the origin of an African working class: Lourenço Marques, 1870–1962'. Boston University African Studies Center Working Papers 13.

Périn-Hockers, Maryse, 1959. *L'absentéisme des travailleurs africans et l'instabilité des enterprises de la région d'Elisabethville 1957–58.* Brussels, Centre d'études des problèmes sociaux indigenes. Memoires, 3.

Perrings, Charles, 1977. 'Consciousness, conflict and proletarianization: an assessment of the 1935 mineworkers' strike on the Northern Rhodesian copperbelt', *Journal of Southern African Studies*, 4.

1979. *Black Mineworkers in Central Africa.* London, Heinemann.

Pfefferman, Guy, 1967. 'Trade unions and politics in French West Africa during the Fourth Republic', *African Affairs*, 66: 213–30.

1968. *Industrial Labor in the Republic of Senegal.* New York, Praeger.

Phillips, Howard and Elizabeth van Heyningen (eds.), 1981. *Studies in the History of Cape Town*, 4. Cape Town, University of Cape Town.

Phimister, Ian R., 1977. 'White miners in historical perspective', *Journal of Southern African Studies*, 3: 187–206.

Phimister, Ian R. and Charles van Onselen, 1978. *Studies in the History of African Mine Labour in Colonial Zimbabwe.* Gwelo, Mambo Press.

Pittin, Renee, 1984. 'Gender and class in a Nigerian industrial setting', *ROAPE*, 31: 71–81.

Plaut, Martin, 1986. 'The Political Significance of COSATU', *Transformation*, 2: 62–72.

Post, Ken, 1977. 'Peasantization in West Africa', in Peter Gutkind and Peter Waterman (eds.), *African Social Studies: A Radical Reader.* London, Heinemann.

Pottier, Johan, 1983. 'Defunct labour reserve? Mambwe villages in the post-migration economy', *Africa*, 53: 2–24.

Powesland, P.G., 1957. *Economic Policy and Labour.* East African Studies 10, East African Institute of Social Research.

Prothero, R.M., 1957. 'Migratory labour from North West Nigeria', *Africa*, 27: 251–61.

Ranger, T.O., 1970. *The African Voice in Southern Rhodesia, 1898–1930.* London, Heinemann.

1975. *Dance and Society in Eastern Africa.* London, Heinemann.

Ranger, Terence, 1978. 'Growing from the roots', *Journal of Southern*

African Studies, 5(1): 99–133.

Raymaekers, Paul, 1963. *L'organisation des zones de squatting*. Brussels, Gembloix.

Rayner, Mary, 1981. 'Slaves, slave owners and the British state: the Cape Colony, 1806–34'. *Institute of Commonwealth Studies*, Societies of Southern Africa seminar paper. London.

Read, Margaret, 1942. 'Migrant labour in Africa and its effects on tribal life', *International Labour Review*, 14: 605–31.

Review of African Political Economy (ROAPE), 1981. Special issue. Kenya: the agrarian question, 20.

Review of African Political Economy (ROAPE), 1984. Special issue on women, oppression and liberation, 27/28.

Rex, John, 1974. 'The compound, the reserves and the urban location', *South African Labour Bulletin*, 1/2: 4–17.

Rey, Pierre-Philippe, 1976. *Les Alliances des classes*. Paris, François Maspéro.

Richards, Audrey (ed.), 1952. *Economic Development and Tribal Change*. Cambridge, Heffer.

Richardson, Peter, 1982. *Chinese Mine Labour in the Transvaal*. London, Macmillan.

Rita Ferreira, A., 1963. *O Movimento Migratório de Trabalhadores entre Moçambique é Africa do Sul*. Lisbon, Junta de Investigações do Ultramar. Centro de Estudos Politicos e Soçiais.

Roberts, B.C. and L.G. de Bellecombe, 1967. *Collective Bargaining in African Countries*. London, Macmillan.

Robertson, A.F., 1982. 'Abusa: structural history of an economic contract', *Journal of Development Studies*, 18: 447–78.

Robertson, Claire, 1984. *Sharing the Same Bowl*. Bloomington, Indiana University Press.

Robertson, H.M., 1934–35. 'One hundred fifty years of economic contact between black and white in South Africa', *South African Journal of Economics*, 2: 403–25 and 3: 3–25.

Rodney, Walter, 1966. 'African slavery and other forms of social oppression on the Upper Guinea Coast in the context of the Atlantic slave trade', *Journal of African History*, 7(3): 431–43.

Roper, J.L., 1958. *Labour Problems in West Africa*. Harmondsworth, Penguin.

Rouch, Jean, 1956. *Migrations au Ghana*. Paris, Société des africanistes.

Roux, Edward, 1964. *Time Longer than Rope*. Madison, University of Wisconsin Press.

Sabot, R., 1979. *Economic Development and Urban Migration in Tanzania, 1900–71*. Oxford, Clarendon Press.

Sachs, E.S., 1957. *Rebels Daughters*. London, Macgibbon and Kee.

Sandbrook, Richard, 1972. 'Patrons, clients and unions: the labour movement and political conflict in Kenya', *Journal of Commonwealth Political Studies*, 10: 3–25.

  1975. *Proletarians and African Capitalism: The Kenyan Case, 1962–70*. Cambridge University Press.

  1977. 'The study of the African "sub-proletariat": a view', *Manpower and Unemployment Research*, 10: 91–101.

Sandbrook, Richard and Jack Arn, 1977. 'The labouring poor and urban class formation: the case of greater Accra' *Centre for Developing Area Studies*, McGill University Occasional Monograph 12.

Sandbrook, Richard and Robin Cohen (eds.), 1975. *The Development of an African Working Class*. London, Longman.

Sanderson, F.E., 1961. 'The development of labour migration from Nyasaland, 1891–1914', *Journal of African History*, 2: 259–71.

Saunders, C.C. (ed.), 1979. *Studies in the History of Cape Town*. Cape Town, University of Cape Town.

Sautter, Gilles, 1967. 'Notes sur la construction du chemin de fer Congo-Océan', *Cahiers d'études africaines*, 7: 220–99.

Schapera, Isaac, 1947. *Migrant Labour and Tribal Life*. London, Oxford University Press.

Scott, Roger, 1966. *The Development of Trade Unions in Uganda*. Nairobi, East African Publishing House.

Seibel, Hans Dieter, 1968. *Industriearbeit und Kulturwandel in Nigeria*. Köln, Westdeutscher Verlag.

Seibel, Helga Renate, 1969. *Die Afrikanerin in Beruf und Familie*. Bielefeld, Bertelsmann.

Sender, John, 1974. 'Some preliminary notes on the political economy of rural development in Tanzania based on a case study in the western Usambaras'. University of Dar es Salaam Economic Research Bureau Paper 74/5.

Senghaas-Knoblach, Eva, 1977. 'The informal sector and peripheral capitalism: critique of a prevailing concept of development', *Manpower and Unemployment Research* 10.

Shea, Philip, 1975. 'The development of an export oriented dyed cloth industry in Kano Emirate in the nineteenth century'. Unpublished PhD thesis, University of Wisconsin.

Shenton, Robert, 1986. *The Development of Capitalism in Northern Nigeria*, London, James Currey.

Shenton, R. and B. Freund, 1979. 'The incorporation of Northern Nigeria into the world capitalist economy'. *ROAPE*, 13: 8–20.

Shivji, Issa, 1976. *Class Struggles in Tanzania*. London/Dar es Salaam, Heinemann.

Sik, Endre, 1966–74. *History of Black Africa*. Budapest, Akadémiai Kiadó.

Silver, Jim, 1978. 'Class struggles in Ghana's mining industry', *Review of African Political Economy*, 12: 67–86.

1981. 'Class struggle and class consciousness: an historical study of mineworkers in Ghana'. Unpublished PhD thesis, University of Sussex.

Simons, H.J. and R. Simons, 1969. *Class and Colour in South Africa*. Harmondsworth, Penguin.

Singh, Makhan, 1969. *A History of Kenya's Trade Union Movement to 1952*. Nairobi, East African Publishing House.

Sitas, Ari, 1984. 'Black workers responses to changes in the metal industry, 1960–80'. Unpublished D Phil thesis, University of the Witwatersrand.

(ed.), 1986. *Black Mamba Rising*. Worker Resistance and Culture, Durban.

Sketchley, Peter and Frances Lappe, 1980. *Casting New Molds*. San Francisco, Institute for Food and Development Policy.

Skinner, E.P., 1960. 'Labour migration and its relationship to socio-economic change in Mossi society', *Africa*, 30: 375–99.

Slater, Henry, 1975. 'Labour and capital in Natal: the Natal Colonization Company, 1860–1948', *Journal of African History*, 16.

Smock, D.R., 1969. *Conflict and Control in an African Trade Union*. Palo Alto, Stanford University Press.

Snyder, Francis, 1981. *Capitalism and Legal Change: An African Transformation*. London, Academic Press.

Stein, Mark, 1977. 'Max Gordon and African unionism on the Witwatersrand, 1935–40'. *South African Labour Bulletin*, 3/3: 41–57.

Stewart, C.C. and D. Crummey (eds.), 1981. *Modes of Production in Africa: The Precolonial Era*. Beverly Hills/London, Sage.

Stichter, Sharon, 1975. 'Workers, trade unions and the Mau Mau rebellion', *Canadian Journal of African Studies*, 9: 259–75.

   1982a. *Migrant Labour in Kenya: Capitalism and African Response*. Harlow, Longmans.

   1982b. 'Women and the labour force in Kenya, 1895–1964'. *Boston University African Studies Center*. Walter Rodney Seminar paper.

   1985. *Migrant Labour*. Cambridge University Press.

Suret-Canale, Jean (ed.), 1974. *Sur le "mode de production asiatique"*. Paris, Editions Sociales.

Surplus People Project, 1984. Report, 6 vols. Cape Town.

Swan, Maureen, 1984. 'The 1913 Natal Indian strike', *Journal of Southern African Studies*, 10(2): 239–58.

Swanson, Maynard W., 1968–69. 'The urban origins of separate development', *Race*, 10: 31–40.

   1976. 'The "Durban system": roots of urban apartheid in colonial Natal', *African Studies*, 35: 159–76.

Swindell, Kenneth, 1985. *Farm Labour*. Cambridge University Press.

Terray, Emmanuel, 1974. 'Long-distance exchange and the formation of the state: the case of the Abron Kingdom of Gyaman', *Economy and Society*, 3: 315–45.

Tettegah, J., 1962. *Towards Nkrumahism: The Role and Tasks of the Trade Unions*. Accra, Ghana TUC.

Thiam, Iba der, 1976. 'La tuerie de Thiès de septembre 1938', *Bulletin de l'Institut Fondamental de l'Afrique Noire-B*, 38: 300–38.

Thomas, Roger, 1973. 'Forced labour in British West Africa: the case of the Northern Territories of the Gold Coast, 1906–27', *Journal of African History*, 14: 79–103.

Thompson, E.P., 1963. *The Making of the English Working Class*. London, Victor Gollancz.

Ticktin, D., 1969. 'The war and the collapse of the South African Labour Party', *South African Historical Journal*, 1: 59–80.

Tosh, John, 1978. 'Lango agriculture during the early colonial period: land and labour in a cash-crop economy', *Journal of African History*, 19: 415–39.

   1980. 'The cash-crop revolution in tropical Africa: an agricultural reappraisal', *African Affairs*, 79: 79–94.

Trachtman, Lester, 1962. 'The labour movement of Ghana: a study of political unionism', *Economic Development and Cultural Change*, 10: 183–99.

Trapido, Stanley, 1970–1. 'South Africa in a comparative study of industrialization', *Journal of Development Studies*, 7.

1978. 'Landlord and tenant in a colonial economy: the Transvaal, 1880–1910', *Journal of Southern African Studies*, 5: 26–56.

Tshibangu, Kabet M., 1974. 'La situation sociale dans le ressort administratif de Likasi pendant la guerre 1940–45', *Etudes d'histoire africaine*, 6: 275–311.

Turrell, R.V., 1987. *Capital and Labour on the Kimberley Diamond Fields*. Cambridge University Press.

Vail, Leroy and Landeg White, 1980. *Capitalism and Colonialism in Mozambique*. London, Heinemann.

van Bruggen, Jochem, 1931. *Ampie*. Amsterdam, Swets and Zeitlinger.

van der Horst, Sheila, 1942. *Native Labour in South Africa*. London, Oxford University Press.

1964. *African Workers in Town*. Cape Town, Oxford University Press.

van Onselen, Charles, 1976. *Chibaro: African Mine Labour in Southern Rhodesia*. Nottingham, Pluto.

1982. *New Babylon: New Nineveh*. Harlow, Longmans.

van Velsen, J., 1960. 'Labour migration as a positive factor in the continuity of Tonga tribal society', *Economic Development and Cultural Change*, 8:265–78.

van Zwanenberg, Roger, 1975. *Colonial Capital and Labour in Kenya*. Nairobi, East African Literature Bureau.

Vaughan, Megan, 1985. 'Household Units in Southern Malawi'. ROAPE, 34: 35–45.

Vercruijsse, Emile, 1979. 'Class formation in the peasant economy of Southern Ghana', *Review of African Political Economy*, 15/16: 93–104.

Vidal, Claudine, 1974. 'Economie de la société féodale rwandaise', *Cahiers d'études africaines*, 14: 52–74.

1977. 'Guerre des sexes à Abidjan: Masculin, feminine, CFA', *Cahiers d'études africaines*, 17: 121–53.

Warmington, W.A., 1960. *A West African Trade Union*. London, Oxford University Press.

Warren, W.M., 1966. 'Urban real wages and the Nigerian trade union movement, 1939–60', *Economic Development and Cultural Change*, 15: 21–36.

1969. Rejoinder. *Economic Development and Cultural Change*, 17: 618–33.

Waterman, Peter, 1973. 'Communist theory in the Nigerian trade union movement', *Politics and Society*, 3: 282–312.

1975. 'The labor aristocracy in Africa: introduction to a debate', *Development and Change*, 6: 57–73.

1976. 'Conservatism among Nigerian workers' in Gavin Williams (ed.) *Nigerian Economy and Society*. London, Rex Collings.

1977. 'The concept of the "semi-proletarianised peasantry": the Lagos dock strike of 1968 and the necessity for reconceptualising the role of the less proletarianised workers in Africa' on Microfiche Interdocumentation. Zug.

1978. 'Consciousness, organisation and action among Lagos portworkers', *Review of African Political Economy*, 13: 47–62.

Watson, W., 1958. *Tribal Cohesion in a Money Economy*. Manchester University Press.

Webster, Eddie (ed.), 1978. *Essays in South African Labour History*. Johannesburg, Ravan Press.

1981. '"Stay-Aways" and the Black Working Class', *Labour, Capital and Society*, 14: 10–39.

1985. *Cast in a Racial Mould*. Johannesburg, Ravan Press.

Weeks, John F., 1968. 'A comment on Peter Kilby', *Journal of Developing Areas*, 3: 7–17, and 1971, 5: 165–74.

1971a. 'Further comment on the Kilby/Weeks debate: an empirical rejoinder'. *Journal of Developing Areas*, 5: 165–74.

1971b. 'The political economy of labor transfer', *Science and Society*, 35: 463–80.

1971c. 'Wage policy and the colonial legacy, a comparative study'. *Journal of Modern African Studies*, 9: 361–87.

Weiskel, T., 1979. 'Labor in the emergent periphery: from slavery to migrant labor among the Baule peoples, 1880–1925' in W.L. Goldfrank (ed.) *The World-System of Capitalism: Past and Present*, 207–33. London/Beverly Hills, Sage.

Welcher, Larry, 1978. 'The relationship between the state and African trade unions in South Africa, 1948–53', *South African Labour*

Bulletin, 4/5: 15–48.

Wellings, Paul and Michael Sutcliffe, 1984. '"Developing" the urban informal sector in South Africa: the reformist paradigm and its fallacies', *Development and Change,* 15: 517–50.

White, Luise, 1984. 'Women's domestic labour in colonial Kenya: prostitution in Nairobi 1909–50' in Cooper, (ed.) (1984).

Wickins, P.L., 1972. 'General labour unions in Cape Town, 1918–20', *South African Journal of Economics,* 40.

   1978. *The Industrial and Commercial Workers' Union of Africa.* Cape Town, Oxford University Press.

Wilentz, Sean, 1983. 'Artisan Republican festivals and the rise of class conflict in New York City, 1788–1837' in Michael Frisch and Daniel Walkowitz (eds.) *Working-Class America.* Urbana, University of Illinois Press.

Williams, Gavin, 1974. 'The political consciousness of the Ibadan poor' in E. de Kadt and G. Williams (eds.) *Sociology and Development.* London, Tavistock.

Wilson, Francis, 1972a. *Labour on the South African Gold Mines.* Cambridge University Press.

   (ed.), 1972b. *Migrant Labour.* Johannesburg, SA Council of Churches, Spro-Cas.

Wilson, Francis et al., 1977. *Farm Labour in South Africa.* Cape Town, David Philip.

Wilson, Godfrey, 1941. *An Essay on the Economics of Detribalization in Northern Rhodesia.* Rhodes-Livingstone Institute.

Wilson, Godfrey and Monica Wilson, 1945. *The Analysis of Social Change.* Cambridge University Press.

Woddis, Jack, 1959. *Africa: The Lion Awakes.* London, Lawrence and Wishart.

Wolpe, Harold, 1972. 'Capitalism and cheap labour-power in South Africa: from segregation to apartheid', *Economy and Society,* 1: 425–56.

Worden, Nigel, 1985. *Slavery in Dutch South Africa.* Cambridge University Press.

Wright, Marcia, 1975. 'Women in peril', *African Social Research,* 20: 800–19.

Yesufu, T.M., 1962. *Introduction to Industrial Relations in Nigeria.* London, Oxford University Press.

Yudelman, David, 1975. 'Industrialisation, race relations and change in South Africa', *African Affairs*, 74: 82–96.

    1983. *The Emergence of Modern South Africa*. Westport, Greenwood Press.

❧ INDEX ❧

Abidjan, 87–88
abolition of slavery, 10
Abu, Katherine, 84
accidents, work, 59
Accra, 88–89
Acheampong, 106
African National Congress (of South
    Africa), 131–32, 135–36
Afrikaners, 115, 119; nationalism, 123; see
    also Boers
age-grades, 5
Agege, 55–56
agriculture and agrarian labour, 1–7, 14,
    23, 32, 34, 36, 43, 63–74, 81–82, South
    African, 113–14, 118, 120, 129, 137,
    141–42
aid, foreign, 76
alcohol, 59
Algeria, 69, 102
Allen, Victor, 63–64
Anglo-American Corporation, 121
Angola, 102, 111, 142
anthropology, 6, 17–18
apartheid, 124–27
apprenticeship, 78, 113
aristocracies, 67–68
Armah, Ayi Kwei, 57
Arrighi, Giovanni, 50–51, 64
artisans, 37–38, 77–78, 123, 135
Arusha Declaration, 18, 64, 101
Asante, 84
Asia, 4, 9, 46, 83, 113
Australia, 67, 115

Bagamoyo, 29
Bantustans, 70
Barth, Heinrich, 28
Baule, 82
Beach, David, 29
beer, 40, 124
Belgian colonialism, 48
beni dancing, 47
Bentum, Benjamin, 105–6, 108

Berg, Elliot and Jeffrey Butler, 19, 103
Berry, Sara, 77–78
Biney, Pobee, 98
blacksmiths, 78
blasting certificate, 117
Boers, 11, 113, 115
Bonis, Jean, 59
Bophuthatswana, 86
Botswana, 95–96, 116
Brazil, 10, 125
brickmaking, 118
Britain and British colonialism, 4, 10–11,
    22, 31, 92, 112, 114–15, 131
Bryceson, Deborah, 86
Bujra, Janet, 56
Bukh, Jette, 141
Bulawayo, 40
Bundy, Colin, 65
Burawoy, Michael, 47, 97
Busia, K.A., 105–6
Buthelezi, Gatsha, 64

California, 115
Cameroon, 82
Cape of Good Hope province, 65, 112–14,
    132
Cape Town, 111
capital goods, 41
capitalism, as a mode of production, 25;
    'colonial,' 37; and class, 45, 58, 60; in
    agriculture, 66–69, 72, 81
capitalists, South African and working
    class, 128
car workers, 132
Caribbean, 8, 10, 92
castes, 28, 78, 88
casual labour, 36
Catholic Church, 48
Cattle Killing, 1857, 112–13
Chaulet, Claudine, 59
Chege, Michael, 56
chibaro, 32

195

child labour, 79; children, 82, 87, 89, 113
Chinese, 115
cigarettes, 40
Ciskei, 33, 126
Clarke, Duncan, 66
class: pre-colonial, 3–5, 12; and slavery, 9;
    analysis, 20–24; consciousness, 23; and
    capitalism, 25; and migration, 36;
    formation, 37; community and culture,
    45–62; the new ruling, 57; struggle, 59;
    and theft, 60; peasantry as, 63–65;
    women as, 82; and politics, 135–36
clerical labour, 38, 86, 91, 129
clientage and clientelism, 35, 56, 70,
    80–81, 91, 104
cloves, 2, 10
coal, 113, 118
Cock, Jacklyn, 79
cocoa, 82
coffee, 34, 67
Cohen, Robin, 23, 59
Cold War, 18, 93
colonial capitalism, 37, 80–81
colonial era, 12–18, 31–43; culture, 47–48,
    60; and trade unions, 91–94; in South
    Africa, 112–14, 139
Colonial Office, 92
colour bar, 123; *see also* racism
Coloureds (South Africa), 122, 134
Comintern, 21
Communism, 21, 45–46; Party of South
    Africa, 132, 136
community and class, 17, 39, 45–62, 108
compounds, 49, 116
concentration (South African capital),
    121–22
Congo; Free State, 13; Basin, 27; Belgian,
    40, 60; *see also* Zaire
Congress of Non-European Trade Unions
    (CNETU), 131
Congress of South African Trade Unions
    (COSATU), 133–36
Conrad, Joseph, 13
consciousness, 23
conscripted labour, 31
Conservative Party (UK), 92
conservatism, worker, 57
consumer goods industries, 131
Convention Peoples' Party (Ghana), 53,
    97–100, 105
Cooper, David, 95–96
Cooper, Frederick, 36, 68
copper, 14; and Copper Belt, 16–18, 39,
    42–43, 59–60, 97, 104
cotton, 34, 71
Council of Unions of South Africa, 133
craft production, 78–79, 84, 88, 122
Crisp, Jeff, 52–53, 97, 105
Cuba, 10

Dagoretti, 56
Dakar, 40, 87
Dar es Salaam, 37, 93, 101
Dawn Broadcast, 99
decentralisation, industrial, 126
DeLange Commission, 127, 130
dependency, 8
depopulation, 8–9
Depression, Great, 40
detribalisation, 17
development, economic, 8, 76–77; and the
    state, 95, 107; and labour, 139–43
diamonds, 14, 29–30, 100
differentials, wage, 38, 52, 91
differentiation, peasant, 56
dockworkers, 36, 38, 51–52, 91; *see also*
    stevedores
domestic labour, 79, 87, 89–90, 119, 124,
    129
Downing of the Tools, 101
drought, 3, 13
drugs, 59
'dual economy,' 36–37
Durban, 118, 126, 132

East Africa, coast, 2, 4, 37–39, 66, 73
East London, 126
'economy of affection,' 3–5
education, 44, 57, 99, 127, 129–30,
    135
Egypt, 4, 5, 102
elders, 5–6
Elkan, Walter, 16
Engels, Friedrich, 22, 45
Epstein, A.L., 17
Etherington, Norman, 11
Ethiopia, 5
Etienne, Mona, 82
Eurocentric, 46
Europe, 8, 46, 83, 87, 111
exclusiveness, labour, 114–15, 123–25

family, *see* household, kinship
Fanon, Frantz, 79–80
farms, state, 141–42
Federation of South African Trade Unions
    (FOSATU), 132
feminist scholarship, 5, 85
Fetter, Bruce, 48–49
feudalism, 69–70
Finley, M.I., 27
fishing, 73
Foevie, D.K., 99
forced labour, 12–14, 20, 30–32, 64
forestry, 119
free labour, 10, 12, 14–15, 29
French in Africa, 10; colonial Africa, 12,
    31, 37, 70, 92–93
Furedi, Frank, 58

Gambia, 35
garment industry, 119
gender, 122; discrimination, 133; *see also*
　women
Germany, 102
Gezira, 34, 71
Ghana, 13, 20, 28, 43–44, 51–54, 57, 82,
　84–85, 88–89, 95, 97–100, 102, 105–8,
　141; *see also* Gold Coast
Ghana Trade Union Congress, 98, 105–6
Gluckman, Max, 17
Goffman, Erving, 50
Gold Coast, 13, 28, 51–52, 71, 97
gold mining, 6; in Ghana, 43–44, 52–53,
　99, 105–6; in South Africa, 11, 14, 17,
　29, 114–17, 121, 130; in Zimbabwe, 32,
　58–60; trade, 8
Goldberg, Melvin, 60
Gordon, Rob, 49–50
Graves, Adrian and Peter Richardson, 67
Grillo, Ralph, 39
griots, 28
groundnuts, 35
guilds, 78, 88
Guinea, 35, 70, 93
Gutkind, Cohen and Copans, 23–24
Guyer, Jane, 74, 82
Gwala, Harry, 132
Gyaman, 6

Harris, Marvin, 16
Hausa, 4, 5, 27, 83
hawkers, 80
health, 13, 59, 99; industrial 133
Henn, Jeanne, 83
'hidden resistance,' 59
history as discipline, 6, 20
Hodgkin, Thomas, 39
homeland policy, South African, 125
homosexuality, 49
Hopkins, Anthony, 10–11
Horn of Africa, 4
household differentiation and inequality,
　5, 12; resists market, 26; mode of
　production, 81, 83, 85
housing, urban (South African), 127, 129,
　135
Hugon, Philippe, 77
Hyden, Goran, 3–4

Ife, 77–78
Ikeja, 54–55
Iliffe, John, 12, 28
imperialism, European, 7–12, 22
import substitution, 126
inboekselingen, 113
India, 113; Indians, 38, 122, 134
Industrial and Commercial Workers
　Union (ICU), 130–31

Industrial Revolution, 87
industrialisation, 40–41, 54–55, 68, 75;
　industrial workers, 81, 85–86; South
　African, 110–11, 118, 121–22, 125–26,
　128–29, 137, 140
influx control, 125–26
informal sector, 23–24, 55, 75–79, 86–88,
　96, 119, 128, 141
investment outside agriculture, 72
Islam, 54, 83
ivory, 8
Ivory Coast, 81, 87–88
Iyayi, F., 57

jazz, 124
Jeffries, Richard, 51–52, 108
Johannesburg, 124; *see also*
　Witwatersrand

Kadalie, Clements, 131
Kalela dance, 17
Kampala, 39
Kane, Francine, 87
Kano, 28, 53–54, 78
karuwai, 84
Kaunda, Kenneth, 104
Kawawa, Rashidi, 93
Kea, Ray, 28
Kenya, 36, 39, 40, 56–58, 67, 70, 72, 86,
　92, 93, 104, 111, 135
Kenya African National Union (KANU),
　135
Khoisan, 112
Kimberley, 29
Kinshasa (Léopoldville), 40
kinship, 5–7, 17, 64, 78, 81, 83, 85, 87
Kraus, Jon, 98, 100, 105, 108
Kwa Zulu, 64, 126

labour aristocracy, 22, 51, 108, 135
labour control and labour process, 48–50;
　in agriculture, 72–74; on mines, 117
Labour Party (South Africa), 115, 119, 123
Lagos, 35–36, 54–56, 74–75
Land Act (South Africa), 1913, 117, 120
Latin America, 46, 126
Leger, Jean, 50
Leitner, Kerstin, 70
Lenin, V.I., 22
Léopold II, 13
Léopoldville (Kinshasa), 40
Lesotho, 33; 116
Lewis, Jack, 65
Lewis, W. Arthur, 73, 139
Lima, 46
lineage mode of production, 6, 26
Lipton, Merle, 70
Livingstone, David, 11
Lovejoy, Paul, 27

Lubeck, Paul, 54, 57
Ludditism, 24
Lugard, Lord, 14
lumpenproletariat, 79–80
Lusaka, 75

Macmillan, W.M., 14–15
Madagascar, 9
Maize Belt, 120
Makola market, 88
Malagasy Republic, 77; *see also*
　Madagascar
Malawi, 33, 69, 116; *see also* Nyasaland
Mali, 35, 70
Mambwe, 42, 140
marriage, 81, 128–29
Marx, Karl, 22, 45, 87
mass production, 111
Mathare Valley, 56
Mau Mau, 58
Mauritania, 59
Mboya, Tom, 93
mechanisation, 69, 120, 124
Meillassoux, Claude, 81–83
merchants, 12; and slavery, 27; and wage
　labour 34, 113; capital, 78–79; and
　women, 83–84, 88–89; *see also* trade
metal industry, 121
Mexico, 125
Mfecane, 114
Mfengu, 112
Middle East, 10
migrant labour, 14–16; pre-colonial, 30; as
　resistance, 16, 36, 59–60; 33–36, 42–43,
　50, 64, 69–71, 73, 126, 140
mining and miners, 29, 32–33, 37–38,
　43–44, 47–50, 52–53, 58–61, 73, 91, 95,
　99, 100, 105–6, 111, 114–17, 121–22,
　123, 130–31
missionaries, 7
Mitchell, Clyde, 17
Mitidja, 69
mobility, worker, 39
modernisation theory, 20
Mombasa, 36, 37
Moodie, Dunbar, 49
motor mechanics, 78
Mozambique, 16, 29–30, 33, 69, 97, 102–3,
　111, 116, 142
Mwadui, 100
Mwangi, Meja, 57

Nairobi, 40, 56, 58, 75, 86
Namibia, 49–50
Natal, 5, 66–67, 113, 118, 120
National Union of Mineworkers (South
　Africa), 50, 133
nationalism, African, 18–20, 22–23, 51, 92,
　97–102, 129, 132, 135

navétanes, 35
Nguni, 5
Niger, 71
Niger river delta, 2, 27
Nigeria, 13, 19, 27, 35–36, 37–39, 41–42,
　53–57, 60–61, 67–68, 71, 77–78, 83–84,
　92, 94–95, 103–4, 142
Nile valley, 4
Nkrumah, Kwame, 19, 53, 97–100
'non-racialism,' 134
North Africa, vii, 2, 4, 8
nurses, 86
Nyasaland, 33, 131; *see also* Malawi
Nyerere, Julius, 18, 46, 64, 101
Nzula, Albert, 21

O'Brien, Jay, 34, 43
oil boom, 42; cooking, 40
'orderly urbanisation,' 126

Pact government (South Africa), 119
Padmore, George, 21
Pan-Africanism, 21
Parti Démocratique du Guinée, 93
Parti Socialiste Sénégalais, 19
party politics, 18–19, 23, 56, 93, 135–36
pass system (South African), 116, 126
patriarchy, 6, 85–86
patronage, 35; *see also* clientage and
　clientelism
Peace, Adrian, 54–56
peasantisation, 64–65
peasants, 3, 5, 36, 43, 63–66, 71–72, 102,
　116–17, 142
peppers, 7
Perrings, Charles, 59–60
petty commodity production, 60–61,
　78–79, 128
Phimister, Ian, 58–59
Pietermaritzburg, 132
Pittin, Renee, 83
plantations, 66–67, 68, 91, 113
political science as discipline, 20
polygyny, 85
'poor whiteism', 119
Popular Front (France), 92
populism, 57, 96
porterage, 28
Portuguese in Africa, 16–17, 30–33;
　colonies, 40, 116
'post-apartheid' South Africa, 137
postal workers, 38, 91, 119
Potekhin, 21
Pottier, Johan, 42, 140
pre-colonial Africa, 1–7
press, 124
Pretoria, 126
proletarianisation, 14, 22, 43–44, 55, 60,
　63, 90, 120, 137; *see also* working class

prostitutes, 84, 86
public works, 119

Queensland, 67

racism, 47–48, 50, 89–90, 91, 119, 121–23, 133
railway workers and railroads, 38–40, 51–52, 100, 113, 118–19
Rand Revolt, 117
Ranger, Terence, 47
recruitment of labour, 32–33, 35
reproduction, social, 86
Reserves, 116, 119–20, 125
retribalisation, 17
Rhodes-Livingstone Institute, 17
Rhodesia, Northern, 16–18, 40, 60, 97; *see also* Zambia
Rhodesia, Southern, 32–33, 39, 40, 57–58, 66; *see also* Zimbabwe
Rhodesian Native Labour Bureau, 32
rice, 2
Riekert Commission, 127
Rita Ferreira, A., 16
Robertson, Claire, 83, 88
Roman Empire, 2
Ruanda-Urundi, 34
rubber, 13
Rwanda, 4

sabotage, 59
Sahara, 2
Sahel, 2
sanctions to South Africa, 137
Sandbrook, Richard, 23, 104
Saul, John, 50–51, 64
Schildkrout, Enid, 84
Scotland, 46
Scramble for Africa, 7, 11–12
seasonal labour, 68–69, 70
secretaries, 86
segregation, 123–24
Sekondi-Takoradi, 51, 98, 100, 108
self-employment, 55
self-management, 101
semi-skilled labour, 122
Senegal, 12, 18–19, 35, 40, 64, 78, 87
Senegambia, 2
Senghor, Louis Sédar, 19, 64
service workers, 42
Shaka, 5
shangwa, 3
Shanghai, 46
shareholding, 120
Shivji, Issa, 101
Shona, 32
Sierra Leone, 2
Sik, Endre, 21
Silver, Jim, 43, 53, 105, 106

sisal plantations, 42
site-and-service housing, 129
skilled workers, 19, 38–39, 41, 50–52, 56, 61, 70, 80; South African, 122, 127, 130, 131, 137
Skinner, Elliot, 16
slave trade, Atlantic, 2, 7–10
slavery in Africa, 2, 4–6, 9–10, 12–13, 26–27, 28–29, 36, 68, 81, 83
Socialist ideas, 38, 53, 135–36
Socialist International, 19
soft drinks, 40
Sokoto Caliphate, 27
Sombart, Werner, 62
South Africa, 9, 11, 17, 25, 29, 33, 48, 50, 64, 65, 69, 80, 110–38, 140, 143
South African Congress of Trade Unions, 131–32
southern Africa, 33, 48, 65
squatters: rural, 67, 102, 120; urban, 124–25, 126
stabilisation of labour, 69, 107, 123, 128
Stanley, H.M., 11
state: pre-colonial, 5–7; employees, 38, 42; power, 57, 62; colonial, 67; post-colonial, 18–20, 69, 94–96, 103–4, 106–8; and the informal sector, 75; South African, 120–22, 125, 128, 137, 141
stevedores, 28, 35–36
Stichter, Sharon, 39
strikes, 18, 19, 37–38, 51, 94, 95, 100, 103–5, 117, 130–31
subsistence, 1–3
Sudan, 34–35, 43, 71
sugar, 8, 10, 68–69, 97, 113, 118
supervision of labour, 49–50, 115, 117, 122–23
surplus production, 3, agriculture 73–74

Tabora, 29
talakawa, 4
Tananarive, 77
Tanganyika, 34, 93; *see also* Tanzania
Tanganyika African National Union, 100–3
Tanganyika Federation of Labour, 93, 100–1
Tanzania, 4, 18–19, 36, 42, 64, 87, 93, 95, 100–3, 107; *see also* Tanganyika *and* Zanzibar
tariffs, 40, 122
taxation and wage labour, 34, 116
tea, 67
teachers, 39, 86, 91
tenancy, labour, 120
Terray, Emmanuel, 6
Tettegah, John, 98–100, 103
textile industry, 132

theft, 60–61, 107
Thompson, Edward, 46, 53
tin, 60–61
Tosh, John, 74
totalitarian labour control, 49
Touré, Sékou, 93
townships, South African, 123–24, 127–28
trade, pre-colonial, 3; colonial, 7; and industry, 55; and peasantry, 66, 114; *see also* merchants
Trade and Labour Congress (South Africa), 131
Trade Union Congress (UK), 92, 94
Trade Union Congress of South Africa, 131–32, 134
trade unions, 17, 18–20, 38, 59, 89, 91–109, 121; South African, 127, 130–35
Transkei, 33
transport revolution, 118; problems, 135
Transvaal, 17, 29, 134; *see also* Witwatersrand
Tunisia, 2
Turkey, 8, 125

Uganda, 16, 34, 39–40
underdevelopment, 8, 57, 75–76
unemployment, 76, 126
Union Minière du Haut-Katanga, 48
UNIP, 135
United Gold Coast Convention, 97
United States of America, 10, 62, 115
unskilled workers, 39, 61, 115, 119, 130
Upper Volta, 16, 71
urbanisation, 15, 17, 30, 40–41, 43, 47, 50–51, 58, 74–75; of women, 84, 85–88, 91; South African, 118–19, 121–22, 124–26, 135, 137

vagabones, 28
Vail, Leroy and Landeg White, 97
Van Onselen, Charles, 32, 58–59
Van Zwanenberg, Roger, 66
Vichy, 92
Vidal, Claudine, 4, 87–88
vent for surplus, 73

WaBenzi, 57
wage labour, 10, 15; and class, 25; first, 28–29, 30–31; not proletarianisation, 35; and World War II, 37, 55, 61; in

agriculture, 67, 74–75; women's, 81–90; and domestic work, 89; decline, 96, 141
warriors, 28
washerwomen, 124
Waterman, Peter, 35, 57
Watson, William, 16, 42, 140
weavers, 28
West Africa, 4, 10–11, 27–28, 38, 53, 73
West Africans in Sudan, 35
White Highlands, 67
White Luise, 86
whites; workers and settlers, 88; 112–19; 122–23, 129, 130–32, 134–35, 138
Wiehahn Commission, 127, 132
Wilson, Godfrey and Monica, 16
Witwatersrand, 11, 33, 114–18
Woddis, Jack, 21
women: exploited, 5–6, 9, 23; as slaves, 26, 30; as workers, 44; in agriculture, 70, 79, 80, 81–90, 119, 124, 128–29, 137, 142
wood, 8, 68
wool, 113
worker consciousness, 59
working class and nationalism, 21–22; and political parties, 23, 24; formation, 25–43; and industry, 41; community and culture, 45–62; rural, 71–72; politics, 94, 106, 108, 112; black in South Africa, 127; politics in South Africa, 132, 135–38
workers' control, 101–2, 136
World War I, 12–13, 31; World War II, 31, 37

Yaounde, 82
Yoruba, 27, 55, 78
Yudelman, David, 127–28

Zaïre, 13; *see also* Congo
Zambesi valley, 69, 97
Zambia, 16–18, 42–43, 47, 104, 135, 140; *see also* Rhodesia, Northern
ZANU, 135
ZAPU, 135
Zanzibar, 2, 5, 10, 27, 29, 37, 68
Zimbabwe, 3, 29, 41, 95, 102–3; 111; *see also* Rhodesia, Southern
Zulu, 5
Zusmanovitch, 21